C0-ATS-068

THEY MADE
THEIR SOULS
ANEW

The Catholic
Theological Union
LIBRARY
Chicago, Ill.

SUNY Series in Modern Jewish Literature and Culture

Sarah Blacher Cohen, Editor

THEY MADE
THEIR SOULS
ANEW

Ils ont refait leur âme

André Neher

Translated by David Maisel

The Catholic
Theological Union
LIBRARY
Chicago, Ill.

WITHDRAWN

STATE UNIVERSITY OF NEW YORK PRESS

Originally published in France
under the title *Ils ont refait leur âme*
Copyright © 1979 by Editions Stock, Paris

Cover designed by Vivian Berger

Published by
State University of New York Press, Albany

© 1990 State University of New York

All rights reserved

Printed in the United States of America

No part of this book may be used or reproduced
in any manner whatsoever without written permission
except in the case of brief quotations embodied in
critical articles and reviews.

For information, address State University of New York
Press, State University Plaza, Albany, N.Y., 12246

Library of Congress Cataloging in Publication Data

Neher, André.
    [Ils ont refait leur âme. English]
    They made their souls anew / André Neher : translated by David
Maisel.
        p.   cm. — (SUNY series in modern Jewish literature and
culture)
    Translation of : Ils ont refait leur âme.
    Includes bibliographical references.
    ISBN 0-7914-0315-7. — ISBN 0-7914-0316-5 (pbk.)
    1. Judaism—Essence, genius, nature. 2. Judaism—20th century.
3. Wolfskehl, Karl, 1869-1948—Religion. 4. Bloch, Ernst,
1885-1977—Contributions in theology. 5. Schoenberg, Arnold,
1874-1951—Religion.   I. Title.   II. Series.
BM565.N43513 1990
296—dc20

89-38685
CIP

CONTENTS

. . . Universal history can sometimes be hidden away in the pages of lexicons. This is the case with the Hebrew term *teshuva* which is not adequately rendered by its New Testament translation *metanoïa* nor by any expression other than the Hebrew term *teshuva*.*

Franz Rosenzweig

*The term is not adequately rendered by the usual English translations of "return" or "repentance" either.

André Neher, one of the major thinkers of contemporary Judaism, was born in Obernai in 1914 and died in Jerusalem in 1988. He was a professor at the University of Strasbourg before making his home in Jerusalem shortly after the Six Day War. He was the author of more than twenty works, including *Moise et la vocation juive*, *l'Essence du prophetisme*, *l'Exil de la Parole*, and *Jerusalem, vécu juif et message*. Translated into some ten languages, including English, Hebrew, Russian, Japanese, German, and Italian, his work has a world-wide audience.

OPENING CHORDS

Prodigal Sons of Assimilation

Heinrich Heine (1797–1856)

Bernard Lazare (1865–1903)

Heinrich Heine

A lost child of assimilation, Heinrich Heine grew up in the atmosphere of liberty which the armies of the French Revolution and Napoleon had brought to the German Jews of the Rhineland. As an adult, he successively espoused baptism in the Lutheran Church, Hellenic apostasy, and then, once again, socialist utopianism. Desertion, indifference, irony, cynicism, libertinism: These were some of the elements of the Heinean anarchy, which also included some incongruous bits of Judaism. He participated as a Jew in the brilliant Berlin salons, and in Paris, in the glittering ambiance of the Grand Opera and the French dramatic revival, even while denying in his actions and writings the Jewish condition which Fromental Halévy and the actress Rachel were then acknowledging with pride. For Heine, Judaism was not a religion but a misfortune, until the day, that is, when misfortune struck him in the form of a painful and incurable illness. Then, on his sickbed-cum-burial-vault in Montmartre, Heine rediscovered the Bible not as a mere literary text but as the organ of the living presence of his great, silent interlocutor, the God of his childhood. All his previous life was now seen as having led up towards a new outcome: he retracted, he confessed. This was a classic case of a Jewish *teshuva*, which for Heine and his readers represented something ineffable which as poet and thinker he was able to express with the accents of Job.

Paris 1851.

RECANTATION I

"I have a confession to make: useless to torture myself any further. Yes, I admit to having returned to God like a lost child. . . . Is it a sense of wretchedness which has forced me to go back? Perhaps the motivation is, after all, not so wretched. What has overcome me is the nostalgia for Heaven."

1852

RECANTATION II

"With regard to my illumination, I owe it quite simply to the reading of a book. A book? Yes, an old book, quiet and modest—as modest as nature and just as natural. A book which is steeped in everyday life and appears to make no demands, like the sun which warms us and the bread which sustains us, a book which gives us a look which is as intimate, as blessed and as benevolent as that of an old grandmother who reads that book with her dear lips atremble and her spectacles on her nose, the book which is called quite simply *the* Book—the Bible."

Bernard Lazare

Another lost child of assimilation, Bernard Lazare grew up in the atmosphere of liberty which the French Third Republic had inherited from all the political systems—empires, monarchies, republics—which had succeeded one another since the establishment of the First Republic a century earlier. There was a total liberty, to such a degree that the young lawyer who had come up from Nîmes to Paris was able to throw himself into the absolute utopia, that of anarchy. He recalled his Jewish origins only in order to put them on trial, to arraign them and condemn them in the first part of a study of anti-Semitism inspired by the anti-Semitic teachings of Edouard Drumont.

Suddenly, the Dreyfus Affair erupted. Bernard Lazare became its prophet, in the spirit of pure prophecy. He was the first to sense, to proclaim, to cry out that Dreyfus was not accused of treason because of any serious suspicions against him, but because he was Jewish. Everyone knew that Dreyfus was innocent. His crime was simply to be Jewish.

Theodore Herzl reacted by writing *The Jewish State*. Bernard Lazare went over to Zionism, but also had another destination. Sick in Paris like Heine, some fifty years after him, he began an uncompleted work of *teshuva:"Le Fumier de Job"* (Job's Dunghill).

Paris 1902–1903

" . . . One day I awoke from a dream. I had lived in the midst of a people and had thought myself to be of the same blood. I had been brought up to rejoice only in its joys, to grieve only at its pains; its soil was my soil, its sky—its sweet sky which I loved—I could not have imagined any lovelier. I thought myself to be the brother of those who were around me, but the day when I awoke I was told that I belonged to another blood, another soil, another sky and another fraternity. I awoke a Jew, but I was ignorant of what a Jew was . . . "

1890?

"I am a Jew, but what is that? Am I no longer a man because I am Jewish? What is it to be a Jew? I have no idea. . . . "

1903

"I have considered, I have thought, I have seen: I am a Jew. I have made my soul anew."

The Vertical Irruption

Franz Rosenzweig (1886–1929)

Arnold Schönberg (1874–1951)

Franz Rosenzweig

BERLIN, OCTOBER 11, 1913.

A young Jew of twenty-seven years, a typical representative of the brilliant German intelligentsia of the early twentieth century, passed through the entrance of a Berlin synagogue. He was aware that the service would begin with Kol Nidre and last throughout the twenty-four hours of the holy day of Yom Kippur, but he was even more conscious of the fact that, when those twenty-four hours were over, he would pass through the entrance of the church where his sponsor Rudolf Ehrenberg, himself a converted Jew, awaited him for baptism. The decision seemed logical and irreversible.

This young Jew, indeed, had almost died at the age of twenty from an immersion in Nietzschean nihilism and the doctrine of perpetual recurrence which creates a vicious circle, in the deterministic materialism that leads to despair and in the Wagnerian "twilight of the gods" which brings one to suicide. Having been born a Jew was no help: He was entirely assimilated into the surrounding German environment and had been brought up in almost total ignorance of Jewish tradition, whether religious, philosophical, or social. Religious tradition? Merely a few vestigial scraps, among which emerged the name of Yom Kippur, the only day of the year when his parents went to synagogue. Jewish philosophy? Never heard of it. Judaism was not a religion, it was a misfortune. As Heine had said long before: How could Judaism elaborate a system of thought? Social destiny? Even the Dreyfus Affair did not make this young Jew feel "concerned."

Those who took him out of this impasse were members of his family, cousins with strong personalities, nourished, like him, on Feuerbach, Nietzsche, and Wagner, who had found a way out of their desperation: salvation through conversion to Christianity. Under their influence this young

11

Jew took a turn for the better, found his faith—the Christian one—and arranged for his baptism to take place the day after Yom Kippur.

If he had decided to go to a Yom Kippur service first, it was first of all out of intellectual honesty. He did not wish to leave Judaism, of which he was ignorant, without having sampled it, and he wanted to enter Christianity like Jesus, the apostles, and the first Christians, as a Jew, for like these others nineteen centuries before, he too had been born Jewish. His baptism was not to be a *new* birth but the consecration of his unique, ineffaceable Jewish birth. He would have liked to have accompanied his parents on their annual pilgrimage to their town of origin, Cassel, but his mother, fully aware of her son's intention of undergoing baptism, did not permit this ambivalent wavering, this comedy of entering the synagogue only in order the better to leave it. "There's no room for renegades in *our* synagogue!" she said. It was for that reason that, alone and unknown to anyone, the prospective renegade went to Berlin, to a synagogue unconnected with any memory, any presence, or even the slightest association with his parents or his ancestors.

He was unknown, except to God. He was alone, yet supported by a community which welded him, despite himself, to a destiny. Something happened. Those twenty-four hours of Yom Kippur—a day of prayer, fasting, and of "return to God, Israel, and myself"—had been enough to transform this young Jew from top to bottom, to overturn him. After the Ne'ila, twenty-four hours after Kol Nidre, he began a long letter which he sent a few days later to the cousin who was to sponsor his baptism: "I'm sorry to disappoint you," he said, "but I am remaining a Jew."

He had had the same experience as Saul in the Bible, but in reverse: He thought he had discovered the kingdom of the Son, but what he found were the simple old asses of his Father.

This "returner to the fold" was Franz Rosenzweig: he died young. But in the fifteen years of life that remained to him he achieved the tour de force not only of having fashioned out a completely Jewish existence but of leaving behind him a philosophical legacy which makes him, together with Martin Buber, the major Jewish religious thinker of the first half of the twentieth century.

Arnold Schöenberg [sic]

On July 24, 1933, Rabbi Louis-Germain Lévy of the *Union libérale israëlite,* 24 rue Copernic, Paris, drew up the following document in his community's notepaper:

On the twenty-fourth of July 1933, M. Arnold Schöenberg [sic], born in Vienna on September 13, 1874, presented himself before us (Louis-Germain Lévy, Rabbi of the *Union libérale israëlite,* 24 rue Copernic in Paris), in order to express his formal desire to return to the community of Israel.

After having been given this present declaration to read, M. Arnold Schoenberg stated that it truly expressed his thought and intentions.

Written in Paris in my study, 24 rue Copernic, the twenty-fourth of July 1933.

Read and approved:
Arnold Schoenberg   Louis-Germain Lévy, Rabbi

Witnesses:
Dr. Marianoff
Marc Chagall

This is a rare document, perhaps the only one of its kind in the long history of the Jewish people. Rabbi Louis-Germain Lévy explained to the prospective returner that Jewish religious law does not recognize "desertion": A Jew, even if converted to another religion, remains Jewish, and there is no need for a special ceremony to mark the return of the renegade to the Jewish fold. But Arnold Schönberg insisted. Born a Jew and converted to Protestantism, he wished his return to Judaism to be consecrated by a religious act, solemn, grave, and at the same time public, a sort of wedding, in the presence of two witnesses and in front of a rabbi, as is customary in the Jewish rites of marriage. The rabbi finally agreed, thus endowing history with this poignant and original document.

What a contrast with the Rosenzweig episode in Berlin twenty years earlier! Then, the drama concerned someone who was solitary and unknown, an individual whose Jewish identity would only be asserted following that Yom Kippur of 1913.

Here in Paris in 1933, on the other hand, the hero of the episode was a world-famous figure, for already the name of Arnold Schönberg was indissociable in the history of contemporary music from the dodecaphonic (twelve-tone) revolution. Since Richard Wagner no composer had revolutionized the mathematics of sounds to the degree that Schönberg had. And, apart from this central figure, one of the two witnesses was Marc Chagall, as famous in the pictorial arts as Schönberg was in music. The scene was thus not played out in the anonymous intimacy of a Jewish soul, as in Berlin in 1913, but in full view of the world of universal culture, of which some of the participants were the conscious and recognized representatives.

Had Arnold Schönberg wanted this complete exposure?

To be sure, he had not felt the need for it in order to allay any condition of inner anxiety. Converted to Christianity in 1898, Arnold Schönberg had never ceased to consider himself, to conduct himself, and to create his work as a Jew, but the coming to power of Hitler in 1933 now obliged him to legalize his break with Christianity. His return to Judaism did not mark a stage in his personal religious development but was intended, rather, to proclaim to the world, to whom his name already belonged, that, in face of the rising tide of anti-Semitism drawing from the sources of Richard Wagner, Arnold Schönberg, the twentieth-century equivalent of Wagner, proudly affirmed his return to the Jewish community which he had momentarily left—a return which, for him at any rate, could not be only social or political, but had to take place in the context of a religious act within the synagogue.

The Challenge of the Holocaust

Karl Wolfskehl (1869–1948)

Benjamin Fondane (1898–1944)

Karl Wolfskehl

Until the autumn of 1933, Karl Wolfskehl had drunk plentifully, in large drafts, at the sources—all the sources—of the Germanic soul. Under the spell of Stefan George, he, like his master, had fashioned poems in a German idiom heavy with Wagnerian symbolism, and he had restored for the modern reader the medieval epic cycles which Wagner had incorporated into his musical philosophy. In short, he had been a Jewish vassal of the domain of the eternal Reich which extended from the Rhine to the Vistula and from the Baltic to the Adriatic, and, with all this, he had forgotten the God of Israel. Worse: He had forgotten that God, for His part, had not forgotten him. And now, behold, that in the midst of his service of idols, God laid hold of him to serve Him and Him alone.

> Lord, you look for me over and over,
> Whenever I cower for cover.
> Your shimmer darts through every cranny,
> And then I know you want me . . .
>
> *The Voice:*
> Yes, yes, and yet alas!
> You saw Me here and everywhere,
> But did you feel My finger,
> Feel that I forced you towards Myself?
> You thought to find me in the worm, the leaf,
> In every pebble smoothed in surf,
> In every bound and glinted ball,
> In call and echo of the call.
> But that was not the course of God—

I am not meant to be found . . .
I, spark, leap from and into self . . .
I am I, only I,
And want you,
You alone:
Because of this, I brought you sorrow cloyed
With bliss, because of this I wrenched you free,
Today you stand before me stripped and void,
Today I have you unalloyed!

Benjamin Fondane

Until the summer of 1940, Benjamin Fondane had drunk plentifully, in large drafts, at the sources—all the sources—of the Latin soul. Having come from his native Romania to Paris he had, like his mentors, fashioned poems out of symbols, retraced the path of Rimbaud and Verlaine, confronted his Latin soul with the Germanic dream of Hegel, frequented Shestov, and loved Europe, France, Paris, the Latin Quarter, and the Seine while sometimes sensing with a certain irony and bitterness that at bottom he was only a wandering Jew. But, during the rout of the exodus of June 1940 when the whole of France gave way, disconcerted, under the impact of Hitler's jackboot, the Jew Fondane found the wandering suddenly took on a sense and the rout became a route where the forgotten God lay in wait for him.

> I fall on my knees, and I weep and I cry
> In a tongue I have forgot, but
> Remember in Thy fearful nights of wrath—
> Adonai Elohenu, Adonai Ehod!

> . . . Thou knowest that when all will be stilled
> Upon earth and in the heavens
> We shall have forgotten Thee. Thou knowest, even now,
> That even the hidden memory of my prayer
> Will fill me with embarrassment. I shall reproach Thee
> For having heard it; I shall reproach myself
> For having uttered it. Thou knowest, I have other gods
> Than Thee—secret, treacherous!
> But here, on the road, in disaster and in

Chaos, there is no other God. Thou art alone!
Terrible, Flaming, Merciful, Unique!

Thus, with a decade between them, two Jews hunted by the swastika sensed and declared, each in his own language but with the same biblical force of poetic expression, that the mort had been sounded not by Amalek but by the shofar of God—the shofar of the God of Israel and of Jerusalem, before Whom had been broken into a thousand miserable fragments the great idols, hitherto worshipped, of Europe and the West; the shofar of the jealous God in search of each of His own, of the God who lay in wait on the crossroads of history to lay hands on His deserters and held them now before Him, never again to let go of them.

These two Jews accepted this duel, this face-to-face or, rather, soul-to-soul combat down to the very last breath, which one of them, Karl Wolf-skehl, breathed as a voluntary exile at the furthest remove from Europe, in New Zealand, in 1948, and the other, Benjamin Fondane, at the furthest remove from humanity, in the gas chambers of Auschwitz on October 2, 1944. Until these final moments, these two, who probably never knew one another, were united by one and the same conviction: Namely, that God had drawn them into His jealous solitude and that it was with Him that they would henceforth live and die, all links with their previous existence having been shattered.

The Challenge of Eretz Israel

Aaron Abraham Kabak (1880–1944)

The Nazir of Jerusalem (1890–1972)

Aaron Abraham Kabak

It was a burning night in Palestine in 1930. The date was close to that of the beginning of the Shoa (Holocaust), but the event had no connection with anything that was taking place outside. It was in the innermost depths of his soul that everything happened in one single night for Aaron Abraham Kabak.

Born near Vilna in 1880, he was educated in Turkey, Germany, France, and Switzerland, and finally settled in Jerusalem in 1921. Very rapidly, this teacher in the Rehavia High School became one of the most celebrated novelists of the new school of Hebrew literature. His work illustrated its essential characteristics: secularism, socialism, free thought, faith in man and the soil, and in the Jewish homeland which was to be built on the foundations of a universal and profane culture. The religion of his forefathers was no more than a childhood memory, thrust into the back of his mind and soon forgotten.

What happened during that burning Jerusalem night? An inner tempest, concerning which Kabak remained silent until his death in 1944. He continued his literary work, making it broader and deeper, but from that night onwards he again took up the tallith, the tefillin, the prayerbook, frequentation of the synagogue and the study of the Bible, the Talmud, and the Masters of the sacred Kingdom which now became the dwelling-place of this secularized Zionist Jew whom a secret dialogue with God had brought back to the Torah, the mitzvot, and the yoke of religious observances accepted in light and joy.

The Nazir of Jerusalem

It was a burning night in St. Gallen, Switzerland in 1915. The incident happened during the First World War, but the event had no connection with anything that was taking place outside. It was in the innermost depths of his soul that everything happened in one single night for David Cohen.

Born in Russia in 1890, he ran away from his yeshiva, the Talmudic academy, in order to savor universal philosophy. He imbibed Socrates, Plato, Descartes, Kant, Hegel, Schopenhauer, and Nietzsche, and his thirst was still not quenched. At a loss, he sought some intellectual or spiritual anchorage and traveled all over Europe. In Switzerland, he was advised to go and consult Rav Kook. Rav Kook was the Chief Rabbi of Jaffa (after the war, he was to become the Chief Rabbi of Palestine), but the war was holding him in Switzerland.

David Cohen was put up in Rav Kook's residence in St. Gallen. Chance had assigned him a room adjacent to that of Rav Kook whom he was to see the next day.

But before the sun rose, David Cohen heard Rav Kook saying—or rather chanting—aloud through the partition the traditional Jewish morning prayers. He awakened the cockerel, the sun, mankind and the cosmos, so intense, fervent, and powerful was his voice. He also awakened David Cohen. When a few hours later Cohen presented himself before Rav Kook, he already knew he had found his Master.

David Cohen did, in fact, become a disciple of Rav Kook. The two men never again left one another and they returned to the Land of Israel at the end of the war. David Cohen settled in Jerusalem and made a vow never again to leave the holy city. He also made a Nazaritic vow: total vegetarianism, hair untouched by scissors, long periods of silence, and asceticism.

After Rav Kook's death in 1935, David Cohen became universally known as "Rav Hanazir," one of the outstanding figures of Jerusalem religious life. The reunification of Jerusalem in 1967 enraptured him and confirmed him in his messianic expectations.

Part One

DIALECTIC OF THE JEWISH CONDITION

To be a Jew is above all to see oneself as related to a historical enigma, whether one recognizes it as rooted in transcendence, whether one insists on denying it or whether one takes it upon oneself . . .

Eliane Amado Lévy Valensi

1

The Knots and the Tensions

THE JEWISH STATEMENT:
AN ESSENTIAL CONTRADICTION

In contesting the Jews' claim simultaneously "to be like the others and to be nevertheless different," and in refusing them these "two contradictory things" in the name of reason, justice, and history, Ernest Renan contested the very essence of Judaism and denied the Jews the secret of their existence. The Jewish statement is essentially a contradiction (Latin *contradictio*, counter-statement). "Nothing can be added to the raw observation that here the antithetical becomes the essence," said Karl Wolfskehl, and without in any way detracting from its rawness, he illustrated the observation with a few paradoxes in which the Jewish concept of the divine shows a similar ambiguity to that of the human. "Does Judaism live in a dwelling or out in the open?" he asked. "Is it faithful or renegade, chosen or rejected? The divine has never ceased to be at odds with it and at the same time has never ceased to dwell with it: what a unique static situation, what a unique dynamics! Its paths are innumerable, its goal obscure. Its outward-directed action is immeasurable, its solitude infinite. . . . The natural sciences no less than the historical are bewildered at this problem."

This problem of an *essential* antithesis is indeed unusual. It comes down to the recognition that in its spirit and development Judaism is molecular, bi-polar, two-dimensional: the religious and the national, the sacred and the secular, identity through the vertical definition of a divine covenant and identity through horizontal membership of a community are inseparable, indissociable, or at any rate, so they ought to be. The Jew is a Gordian knot. A painful tension arises when some Alexander within him or outside of him applies a sword to this knot, this knotted "ought to be," in an attempt to slice it apart.

The French Revolution, and Napoleon after it, attempted precisely this. To a very great extent they succeeded in fissuring one of the Jewish molecules. The "Jewish nation"—to use a term which hitherto had designated both the Jewish religion and the Jewish people—was disbanded. Only one of the atoms of the split molecule survived: the religious atom. The price one had to pay did not appear to be excessive. The Jew retained the Jewish religion with the very fullest freedom of worship, and as for the Jewish national atom, it was not entirely lost. Some element of nationality was granted the Jew, but it was another nationality: French, English, German. . . .

Here a reference to Littré is instructive (Littré is a famous nineteenth-century dictionary which still remains the standard work of reference for the French language). Under the word Jew one finds two senses:

1. Someone who belongs to the Jewish people, to the people that formerly inhabited Palestine.

2. Someone who professes the Jewish religion. A Jew is a Frenchman, a German, an Englishman, etc., who professes the Jewish religion.

It seemed a fair enough exchange. The land of France into which one was henceforth integrated, and those who had died for it, appeared more real and concrete than a vague, abstract association with a nation which had its martyrs, certainly, but which had no land.

The Jews could have continued to have lived on this basis if the tension had not increased in another of the knots of Jewish problematics: the polarity of what Wolfskehl called the "immeasurable outward-directed action" and the "infinite solitude." It was the fissure of this other molecule which put the life of the Jews in danger in the nineteenth century.

For the problem of the Jew was not the same as Hamlet's. "Not to be" is not Jewish: It is the very negation of Jewishness. Allied as he is with the Eternal Being, the Jew is eternal also. Thus, it is not a matter of "To be or not to be." What *is* Jewish, on the other hand, is the tension between "being for oneself" and "being with the others."

THE DIALECTICS OF "BEING FOR ONESELF" AND "BEING WITH THE OTHERS"

Remaining in one's dwelling place, existing in solitude: This is one Jewish attitude, exemplified in the typological idea which the Bible put in the mouth of a foreign observer, the Midianite prophet Bileam. His original intention was to curse, to make the Jew into the pariah of history, but under divine constraint he was forced to bless and to admit that the Jew was not a pariah but that which is *unique* in history: "It is a people that dwells

alone and is not counted among the nations" (Numbers 23:9). This unique-ness forms the chain of Jewish existence, its ontological vocation.
     Within that chain, however, there is the counter-movement: living with others, living in solitude, but not in isolation. Knowing one has a home, but going outside and taking in deep breaths of the air at large, while enriching it with one's own oxygen. That is the would-be condition of Judaism, its utopian condition.
     There are many examples of the interplay and coexistence of "being for oneself" and "being with the others" in Jewish history, Jewish thought, and Jewish existence, beginning with the time of the Bible and lasting throughout the Alexandrian and Talmudic periods and throughout the Middle Ages and the modern period up to the present day. May I be permitted, instead of drawing up an incomplete list of these examples, to refer the reader to two books whose titles or subtitles stress the instructive character of these examples:

André Neher: *L'Existence juive, solitude et affrontements* (Jewish Ex-
     istence, Solitude and Confrontations)
Jacob L. Talmon: *The Unique and the Universal*

     Talmon and I chose these titles and subtitles in the nineteen-sixties, but at the beginning of the twentieth century Bernard Lazare summed up this dialectic in a memorable phrase that called attention to both the superb beauty of this Jewish dual vocation and the terrible dangers which are in it: "To participate in the work of mankind while remaining oneself."

TAKING THE SAME PATH AS EVERYONE ELSE

To join other men with a vigorous revolutionary cooperation in laboring on earth is the physical Jewish *vocation,* but it has its metaphysical reverse side which is that, at the very moment when the Jew is seen by others as someone like themselves, God looks upon him in a way which makes him, conversely, into something other than a man in the earthly, technical, banal sense of the word. This is the metaphysical Jewish *mission,* rooted in the physical. It is a mission of sensitizing history. Humanity would be amorphous if the Jew were not omnipresent, inside everything, like a heart carrying the divine sap through the social organism. It is a mission of marking time. On the sundial of the ages, each of which marks a different hour of humanity, the Jew shows the permanent hour of God. It is a cautionary mission. On a road signposted with religious, political, social, and economic systems, the Jew sets up the placard "not yet" and "still to be accomplished,'' and on the ''final'' placard of history he places an arrow pointing towards the ''tomorrow which still may be.''

Or, seen in the opposite perspective, suffused with the prophetic halo, aglow with the divine gaze continually cast upon him, separated in the study and practice of the Law, standing upright at attention in silent prayer which sets him apart from the entire world except from Jerusalem towards which his whole body and soul are turned, the Jew is nonetheless a labourer upon the surface of the earth, adapted to the rhythms of human time and ready to take up arms in defense of everyone's rights and to use them on the barricades of universal justice.

''The Jews,'' said Charles Péguy, ''since the dispersion appear to offer an example—and the only one—of a spiritual race pursued, scattered and driven forward without the support of a temporal and especially military armour, and without the support of a state and particularly an army.

''Secondly, however . . . in this respect and to this degree, the Jewish dispersion has also taken on the forms which everyone else has and has entered into the world which everyone has entered. . . . Israel in the end took, and had to take for its dispersion, the world which Rome had created, the world which everyone else has taken. . . . ''

THE DANGER: MOVING FROM PARTICIPATION TO ALIENATION

The danger may be easily detected. Through insisting on participation with others, one runs the risk of losing oneself. The desire to be similar leads from similarity to assimilation. There are numerous variations, for the historical circumstances in which the emancipation of the Jews took place were infinitely various, and infinitely various, likewise, are the ways in which the Jews have reacted to these conditionings. Assimilation through a change of place of residence or costume, the adoption of a non-Jewish surname—all this amounts to a resemblance acquired through disguise. Then there is assimilation through an excision of whatever remained Jewish in the molecule split by the Emancipation, that is, in the religious atom. That is to say, a resemblance achieved through a reform of religious observance: a displacement of the Sabbath to Sunday, the substitution of the European national language for the liturgical Hebrew, the transformation of the synagogue into a church and the rabbinate into a clergy, a refusal to mix religious and social affairs, and the adoption of a position of political neutrality with a consequent diversification of political options. Henceforth, when these policies are followed, the Jew no longer adopts a purely Jewish position in the human struggle but is to be found in the extremes and in all the intermediary positions between the left and right, with the unconscious desire to be in the place where one is overwhelmed by the majority—in the center.

The final stage of this process is quite simply the abandonment of the Jewish atom—assimilation through conversion, either to another religion (the Christianity dominant in Europe) or to a secular doctrine: socialism, Marxism, humanism, nihilism, or any "ism" whatsoever providing only that the "Juda" element is eliminated. Even Zionism, in the beginning (Pinsker in *Auto-emancipation*, Herzl in *The Jewish State*) did not lay the emphasis on the "Zion"—which would have meant attaching the "ism" to Jewish fidelity—but placed the accent on the "ism" which was then preceded by the term "nation." "Jewish nationalism" signified the Jews as a nation like the others, having a state like the others, making this state into a state like the others.

I said the final stage, but in fact, it is the final stage but one. The final stage of assimilation is to convert to the "ism" which does not simply obliterate the "Juda" element in Judaism by voidance or substitution but by Judaicide. Judaicide is the ultimate conclusion of the Jew wanting his Jewishness to be "like the others," for the others draw the Jew into their nets in order to make him disappear from the scene of history. Those Jews who are themselves anti-Jewish and anti-Semitic carry out this act of disappearance with the complicity of the others with whom they wish to identify in every respect, even if it entails the masochistic action of ceasing to exist.

THE DISSYMMETRICAL CHARACTER OF THE NINETEETH CENTURY

Nineteenth-century Jewish history is "sandwiched," as it were, between two solemn assemblies: the Grand Sanhedrin in Paris in 1807 and the first Zionist Congress in Basle in 1897. These two assemblies ninety years apart seem, in their granite majesty, to display the positive orientation of that century, a true "antipodes" of the long preceding centuries of the Jewish Diaspora.

Having been extracted from their physical and moral ghetto by the shining grace of the French Revolution, the Jews were free—almost everywhere in practice, but where they were not, they were free as far as circumstances allowed. They had full citizenship (acquired or promised) in their respective lands of the Diaspora, and in addition, the realization of the immemorial dream of "next year in Jerusalem" now entered the bounds of the possible. "I have founded the modern Jewish State at Basle," said Theodore Herzl, just as ninety years earlier Abraham Furtado believed he had created the "modern Jew" in Paris. The two assemblies apparently formed the prelude and the climax of a glorious symphony.

In fact, however, they were points of discord and contradiction in a pattern of tension which ran through the nineteenth century from end to end and, far from bringing the Jew into a state of harmony, revealed him as being wrenched apart like a flayed animal.

In 1807 the Grand Sanhedrin decided on a religious definition of the Jew. In 1897 the Zionist Congress decided on a national definition. In 1807 the Grand Sanhedrin reached its conclusions in answer to questions put to the Jews from the outside, represented at that moment by Napoleon Bonaparte. In 1897 the Zionist Congress arrived at its program in answer to the questions put to the Jews from the inside, represented at that moment by Theodore Herzl. But whose was the daring scalpel which dared to disrupt the essential unity within the Jewish organism of the religious and national elements? What was the mysterious mechanism which caused the Jewish question to switch from an outward-looking orientation to an inward one, whereas, when properly understood, the outside and inside are essentially interconnected? Furthermore, how was it that these two assemblies which sought to represent the Jew in his integrality were denied, ignored, thrust aside, treated with contempt, and declared null and void by the vast majority of Jews who, in 1897, identified neither with the religion nor with the nation, nor with the outside, nor with the inside but with a thousand-faceted otherness in which they recognized themselves although none of these facets had been envisaged either by the decisions of the Grand Sanhedrin nor by the program of the Zionist Congress?

Judged by the criteria we have used so far, the first Zionist Congress, at the end of a century opened by the Grand Sanhedrin, represented a tremendous attempt at repairing the cracks, at recreating the unity of the dismembered Jew. The Sanhedrin had left the Jew only his religious identity. Zionism, without taking that away, restored to him his national identity.

Henceforth, the Jew was once again a member of a people—one which was soon to create its own state like the others but, at the same time, a state not in Uganda or in Argentina but only in Palestine, the Holy Land consecrated by its biblical origins, attuned to the rhythm of the Sabbath and the biblical festivals and marked with the sign of the Jewish particularity.

Henceforth, the Jew was once again someone apart, set aside in his own national state with its national tongue and institutions with biblical roots and, at the same time, a state like the others—a fragile, vulnerable state subject to political, economic, and military vicissitudes.

Henceforth, the Jew was once again at one and the same time a sentinel and a warrior, a soldier and a peasant, but his labor upon the crust of the earth, described by the Hebrew term *avodah*, was both work and prayer.

In the light of the events of the twentieth century, this action of repair initiated by the Zionist Congress of 1897, this apparently harmonious reconstitution of the dismembered Jew, proved to be transient and illusory. There appeared to be a happy conjunction of events following the First World War. It was the full light after the darkness. Reality seemed to overtake the dream. The Jews gained freedom everywhere, even in Russia, and in addition they were able to embody the hope of "next year in Jerusalem" within the political framework of the British Mandate in Palestine.

However, in the same way as the upward movement of the nineteenth century had been countered by a negative force marked by great and tumultuous affairs (the Damascus Affair of 1840, the Mortara Affair of 1858, the Tisza-Eszlar Affair of 1882 and, above all, the Dreyfus Affair of 1894), so the euphoria of the 1920s was shattered by an explosion of greater violence than any that had been known previously—an unexpected explosion, sudden, blinding, and overwhelming: Hitler, the Third Reich, Nazi anti-Semitism, the swastika. The Holocaust, known in Hebrew as the *Shoa*.

2

The "Anti" and Its Masks

There is no need for me to retrace the history of anti-Semitism here. After Jules Isaac, Léon Poliakov, Marcel Simon, F. Lovsky, James Parkes, Renée Neher-Bernheim, Robert Mizrahi, Jacques Givet, Beate Klarsfeld, and so many others have done so, it would be a waste of time and paper. The history of anti-Semitism exists. It is a fact.

But, unfortunately, the existence of this history of anti-Semitism has in no way banished anti-Semitism from history. The latter continues to drag into its foul waters the "anti" decked out with various complements (Judaism, Semitism, Zionism) whose object, however, always remains the same—the Jew—and likewise its objective: his extermination. As long as this goal is not yet achieved, the anti-Semite will not give in. No moral can be drawn from this story, if it is not that its protagonists possess an inexhaustible wardrobe and are always able to find the appropriate mask for their demented role.

FROM THE WITNESS STAND TO THE BOX
OF THE ACCUSED

We know very well that it is "not easy to be Jewish." Péguy said as much when reflecting retrospectively on the Dreyfus Affair. We are aware, also, that, for the Jews, liberty is a burden. "Difficult Liberty" is what Levinas called his penetrating analysis of the problem of emancipation.

But what took place with the entry of the swastika into history was what Péguy suspected lay *behind* anti-Semitism. "You constantly heap contradictory reproaches upon them," he said. "At bottom, what you want is that they should not exist." Yes, that indeed is what lies at the bottom of the contradiction. Everything else is just surface.

In the nineteenth century, during the upward curve of that century, when a Jew was called before the tribunal of humanity, it was as a witness:

37

"Come forward and declare your name."

"My name? Although it is not my family name, I am called Jew, a word which means "one who praises"—a constant celebrator of the One who is, the Only One, the Eternal."

"Your age?"

"My age? Two thousand years more than Jesus Christ."

"Your profession?"

"My traditional profession is as follows: I guarantee the sacred indefeasability of the name of the Law."

"Raise your hand and promise to speak without hatred and without fear, and to say the whole truth."

"I pledge myself to do so with all my heart and soul. I swear to do so before God and men."

"Speak forth, then, with the brevity of your fathers and tell us what you know. . . . "

Joseph Salvador, 1850

Between 1933 and 1945, the Jew, brought before the tribunal with the word JEW stamped on his identity card, a yellow star on his chest, and a number tattooed on his arm, thought he could come forward as in Salvador's day as a witness, but suddenly realized that he had not been called in as a witness. He had been brought before the tribunal of mankind as the accused. This change from witness to accused, from Salvador to Kafka, is a psychological circumstance which made the difficulty of being Jewish even more of a burden.

We should note, incidentally, that this change from witness to accused simply reflects another of the masks of the "anti" in the drama of history. It was a manifestation of the transference of the theological power of the "anti" to its secular power. In making the Jew part of the drama of the Passion, Christian theology, to be sure, was not guilty of any particular charity towards him. Individual and collective massacres signposted the long road of a bloodstained history which began at the very moment when the betrayal of Judas was laid to the account of the Jewish people, henceforth accused of the crime of deicide. We are told that it was only the common Christians—the people, the masses, those ignorant of theological truth—who demanded and perpetuated the death of the deicide people. The learned possessors of the Christian truth knew that the Jewish people, precisely because it was deicide, had to survive and to go through history with the malediction of having to wander, in the state of forfeiture of the blind synagogue, in order to serve until the end of time as a witness of the drama in which it played the undoubted role of Judas. A Judas-surrogate, the wandering Jew had to endure, but in a scattered and dismembered condition, carrying in a perpetual exile the cross of his loss of status which bore witness to the light of the true cross which he had denied:

"God has thus caused the Church to understand, with regard to its enemies the Jews, wherein His mercy consists," wrote St. Augustine in the 5th century CE, "for, as the apostle says, 'through their fall cometh salvation to the Gentiles' (Romans 11:2). Although they were conquered and oppressed by the Romans, God did not 'slay' them, that is, he did not destroy them as Jews. For, in that case, they would have forgotten and would have been useless as witnesses to what I am speaking of. Consequently, the first part of the prophecy, 'slay them not lest they forget they law' is of small import without the rest, 'scatter them.' For, if the Jews had remained bottled up in their own land with the evidence of their Scriptures and if they were not to be found everywhere, as the Church is, the Church would not then have them as ubiquitous witnesses of the ancient prophecies concerning Christ."

(The City of God 18:46 and 47).

THE CRIME OF EXISTING

It was in the rapid second phase of the trial that the burden became intolerable. It was not the first time that the Jew had been accused in the course of his long history. The Jews had been accused of poisoning wells, of spreading plagues, of being in league with the devil, of being usurers, deicides, elements of social decomposition, traitors. The Jews had been accused of ritual crimes. They had been accused, but they knew that all these accusations were false, completely unfounded. Still now, the Jew moved towards the box of accusation with a conviction of innocence. He attempted to plead, but now he was confronted with a judge who, standing before him, accused him of quite another crime, a crime against which he could bring no proof of innocence, a crime whose guilt one cannot avoid and which can only be expiated by death: the crime of existence.

Jewish existence: solitude or confrontation? The Jewish contradiction: "being with the others" or "being for oneself"? Nothing any longer had any meaning except simply remaining alive, with the accusing addition of the word JEW. With the others or for oneself, alone or in solidarity, oriented outward or inward—all these were now absurdities, hollow words, mere additional data which the judge erases off-handedly, leaving only the menacing two-worded formula: Jewish existence.

. . . Yes, I've been a man like all other men . . .

. . . Yet no!
I was not a man like you . . .

. . . Accused of a crime you did not commit—
The crime of existing . . .

Benjamin Fondane

THE FRUITLESS ESCAPE

When Heine converted to Christianity in 1824, the word anti-Semitism did not yet exist, but the thing was already there in a covert, embryonic way, and one of Heine's most prophetic acts was to have detected, described, and analyzed it in its most aggressive form and to have tried vainly to exorcise it.

Heine's conversion was of no avail. It was not, to be sure, that he expected something from Christianity, but from Germany. To be accepted into its normal cultural environment in that period, an "entry ticket" was required—baptism. But no sooner was that ticket acquired than it was declared to be null and void. Heine, at the dawn of the Emancipation, was one of the first Jews to have experienced the fact that the Jewish condition is irrevocable. *Der nie abzuwaschende Jude* (the unwashable Jew): One is Jewish as one is black. No cleansing can remove the infamous stain. Emancipation or baptism may take away the Jewish badge, remove the physical burden, but they leave intact the Jewish identity and the spiritual burden. They are only ridiculous masquerades. Heine tried both of them, but neither the one nor the other protected him. He continued to receive the full load of insults and threats. He was trapped by the fact of his being Jewish.

Was it possible for him to find any way out of this situation? Heine thought he knew of several, and here again he provided an example of someone who tried various experiments which others imitated, recklessly throwing themselves into the same failures as he did. Did not the secular world open its generous gates to him if he wanted to cross them? No entry ticket, no baptism would do. There was no price that could be paid—above all not that of self-abjuration—which could transform Heine the Jew into a Hellene, a socialist, a communist, or quite simply into a man.

In vain. Throughout all these vicissitudes, the fact of his being Jewish earned Heine distrust, insults, exile, and finally isolation.

It caused thousands of Russian-Jewish communists to be shot on the orders of Stalin.

It caused Marc Bloch, the prototype of the secularized French Jew, to be shot in the France of Marshal Pétain.

For Stefan Zweig, the prototype of the secularized European Jew, feeling himself to be rejected by everyone, there was no solution except suicide.

Another escape route was self-hatred. The *Baths of Lucca* provides an extraordinary record of it. A reply to Platen's anti-Semitism, this pamphlet of Heine's strikes at the adversary, to be sure, but at the same time it constitutes a bitter self-accusation. Heine felt himself to be an accomplice of the Gumpel-Gumpelinos and Hirsch-Hyacinths trapped in their condition as Jews, in their misfortune in being Jewish.

Taken to its extremity, self-hatred led Trotsky to make a special point of sending his fellow Jews to the front as cannon fodder.

Taken to its extremity, self-hatred led the Jew Otto Weininger to suicide.

DID THE "ANTI" HAVE ITS ROOTS IN GERMANY?

Heine's great contribution to our understanding of anti-Semitism is to have established its connection with Germany. In his *History of German Religion and Philosophy* which appeared in 1832, he described the tendency to irrationality which, since the Nibelungen and Martin Luther, was to be found in the major symbols of Germany—the Michel, Troll-Atta, the pointed helmet—as well as in its religious and secular thinkers. Heine foresaw the reawakening of the Germanic gods buried beneath the veneer of Christianity—Wotan, Valhalla, the Walkyries. One day, he said, amidst mighty storms, humanistic culture not only in Germany but in the whole of Europe will collapse under the impact of this rude awakening if it does not prevent it in time. Richard Wagner, Bismarck, William II, and Hitler were all prefigured in this hallucinating vision.

This German irrationality included anti-Semitism (the word itself was in fact invented in Germany some fifty years later) in its most extreme forms. There was the racial form, unalloyed with either theological arguments or economic motivations, but based on birth, blood, and instinct. There was the social form, to whose realization bleating masses, screaming herds, mechanical robots gave themselves up. There was the political form: the "black sect" was a first edition, one century earlier, of the brownshirts. Its members, gathered together in the beer halls of Munich, in a fit of delirium associated the life of Germany with the death of the Jews. They thought of the most fantastic ways of bringing all this about:

The members of the black sect are ideologues who have read everything, and stuff their encyclopedic knowledge into the straitjacket of their brutal stupidity. They are *gründlich* (thorough), critics, historians. They are able to determine with an absolute precision the degree of racial affiliation which in the new order of things will require you to be eliminated. They only discuss the method of extermination.

This was written by Heine in 1829.

These lines can be placed between two texts, one previous to this date and the other subsequent to it. It was not the obscure members of an obscure beer hall coterie which wrote them, but two of the greatest figures of German philosophy and German art. Heine knew these texts and their authors. He had been the disciple of the philosopher at Jena before his exile in Paris, where he was one of the patrons of the artist:

"To grant civic rights to the Jews is possible only on one condition," said the philosopher. "To cut all their heads off in a single night and give them new ones which will not contain a single Jewish thought."

J. G. Fichte, *Beiträge zur Berichtigung des Urteile
uber die französische Revolution*, 1793

"Know that for you there is but one redemption from the weight of malediction which rests on you," said the artist. "The redemption of Ahasuerus, or, in other words—disappearance! . . . "

Richard Wagner, *Judaism in Music*, 1853

When one reads Jakob Wassermann, one can see that Heine's intuition was historically correct. This German-Jewish novelist was a contemporary of the reawakening of the Germanic deities predicted by Heine a century earlier. In 1923, ten years before Hitler came to power, when the future dictator was still but a grotesque clown waving banners with the brownshirts' swastika in the beer halls of Munich (and already writing "Mein Kampf" which nobody then took seriously), and a century after Heine had noted the deliberations of the black-brown sect in those same Munich beer cellars, Jakob Wassermann took stock of his "path as a German and as a Jew." The result was a despairing analysis of the infernal vicious circle in which the Jew had been imprisoned by the "anti" in its German guise. The analysis concluded with a poignant confession which constitutes the vade-mecum of the betrayed Jew:

What should one do?
Vain to adjure the nation of poets and thinkers in the name of its

poets and thinkers. Every prejudice that one believes to be disposed of breeds a thousand others, as carrion breeds maggots.

Vain to present the right cheek when the left has been smitten. This does not move them to thought; it neither touches nor disarms them: They strike the right cheek also.

Vain to interject words of reason into their crazy shrieking. They say: "He dares to open his mouth? Gag him."

Vain to set an example in your life and behavior. They say: "We know nothing, we have seen nothing, we have heard nothing."

Vain to seek obscurity. They say: "The coward! He is creeping into hiding, driven by his evil conscience!"

Vain to go among them and offer one's hand. They say: "Why does he take such liberties with his Jewish obtrusiveness?"

Vain to keep faith with them, as a comrade-in-arms or a fellow citizen. They say: "He is Proteus, he can assume any shape or form."

Vain to help them to strip off the chains of slavery. They say: "No doubt he found it profitable."

Vain to counteract the poison. They brew fresh venom.

Vain to live for them and die for them. They say: "He is a Jew. A Jew he was, a Jew he will remain."

THE "ANTI" HAS ROOTS IN FRANCE

The Dreyfus Affair.

This was the tremendous, heartbreaking, sickening, inconceivable, and yet, for all that, undeniable proof of the element of illusion in Heine's vision. Anti-Semitism is associated with Germany, that is true. But it has deep roots in France. Yes, in France also, O land of liberty!

The French Revolution, the two Empires, the constitutional monarchies, the three Republics, the generosity of a people which lent its "Marseillaise" to all the barricades in the world, beginning with its own on which it planted the Tree of Liberty; the hospitality of Paris—generous also—opening itself up to all the exiles, all the famished, all the outcasts in the world, offering them a roll of bread, a glass of coarse red wine, the synagogue, the rue des Rosiers, Montmartre, liberty; the boundless gratitude, generous also, ultra-generous, of the French Jews and foreign Jews, giving their intelligence and their goodness, their hearts and their brains, their lives and their deaths for the homeland . . .

I have counted you all,
Civilians of yesterday—shopowners, peasants,
Factory workers, tramps whose nest
Is under the bridges of Notre Dame . . .
Frenchmen according to the Rights of Man,
Sons of the barricade and guillotine,
Sans culottes, incorruptible, free,
And Czechs, Poles, Slovaks,
Jews from all the ghettos of the world
Who loved this land, its shade and rivers
And with their death sowed this land,
Frenchmen according to their death.

Benjamin Fondane

. . . all this was not enough to root out here in Paris where, a century earlier, the rights of man came into being, the terrible curse of anti-Judaism, of anti-Semitism, of the "anti" which attached itself to Captain Alfred Dreyfus because he was Jewish. The cry of Dreyfus, "I am innocent!" during the Calvary of his degradation, is the very cry of Jewish innocence. It entered like a sharp scalpel into the soul of the Viennese Jewish journalist Theodor Herzl who was present at the scene. It entered like a sharp scalpel into the soul of the French Jewish anarchist Bernard Lazare. It grew from person to person, searing consciences, summoning to the aid of hounded liberty half of France: Colonel Picquart, Scheurer-Kestner, Charles Péguy, Émile Zola . . . In vain. The other half of France, shouting louder in a collective psychosis close to paranoia, overwhelmed the cry of innocence with the only cry which the anti-Semite knows, wants to know, or is able to know: "Death to the Jew! Death to the Jews!" From the singular form, one crosses automatically to the plural. If one Jew is a traitor, then they must all be traitors, and all those who take up their defense. It is the law of generalization: They must all be exterminated.

"Is Zola guilty?" . . .
The chief juryman got up: "Yes, by a majority."
At the back of the courtroom, there was a new round of applause. M. Émile Zola, referring to this applause, exclaimed: "They're cannibals!"
The President then read out the verdict: "M. Zola is condemned to one year in prison and a fine of three thousand francs."

The Zola trial, stenographic report, Paris, February 28, 1898

Everything now once again became possible. With the Dreyfus Affair, the chapter in Jewish history which seemed to have been definitely closed in 1789 was reopened: The Middle Ages rose once more. To be sure, Dreyfus was rehabilitated in 1906. It is to the immortal honor of France that at the beginning of the twentieth century it again performed the creative gesture which it first introduced into history at the end of the eighteenth century: "Let there be light, and there was light!" A light which shone incandescent, with full strength, in the *union sacrée* of the battlefields of Verdun where the general staff, headed by General Pétain, completely abolished the difference between the Jewish soldier and the soldier who was not, between Alfred Dreyfus and those who were not born Dreyfus or Masse or Isaac.

However, there is a direct, continuous, indestructible link between the French anti-Semitism of the "Affair" and the Nazism of 1933. Pétain, again, finds his place in it. If the year 1906 saw the rehabilitation of Dreyfus, the Jewish Statute of 1940, enacted by the Pétain government in Vichy, was the rehabilitation of Esterhazy, Dreyfus's accuser. It was the green light for the systematic extermination of the Jews of France, born in France or accepted by France—"Frenchmen according to the rights of man" or "Frenchmen through their death"—an extermination which only chance, Providence, the Resistance, and the end of the war prevented from becoming total.

"I have read the decree which states that no Jews can any longer be officers, even those of purely French descent.

"I should be obliged if you would tell me if I should strip of their rank my brother, sub-lieutenant of the Thirty-sixth Infantry Regiment, killed at Douaumont in April 1916; my brother-in-law, sub-lieutenant of the Fourteenth Dragoon Regiment, killed in Belgium in May 1940, and my brother J. F. Masse, lieutenant of the Twenty-third Colonial Regiment, killed at Rethel in May 1940.

"Can I leave my brother the military medal won at Neuville-Saint-Vast with which I buried him? Can my son Jacques, sub-lieutenant of the Sixty-second Batallion of the Mountain Light Infantry, wounded at Soupir in June 1940, keep his stripes?

"Finally, can I be assured that the Medal of St. Helena will not be taken retroactively from my great-grandfather? I wish to observe the laws of my country, even when they are dictated by the invader."

Letter of the lawyer Pierre Masse to Marshal Pétain

(Pierre Masse never received a reply to this letter, unless the answer was his arrest, his deportation, and his assassination in the gas chambers of

Auschwitz. Another reply provided by history: Pierre Masse's niece today lives in Israel).

> To my wife, to my daughter
> Martyrs
>
> Killed by the Germans
> Killed
> Simply because they were called
> ISAAC.
>
> Jules Isaac, dedication of
> *Jésus et Israël*

. . . And if it is necessary, O my God, that I must henceforth carry with me the memory—imaginary, yet obstinately, atrociously present—of that last look, why do you have to punish me through the purity of my love for my country? For I know very well, I sense that something has changed in that love, that perhaps I shall never again be able to think of France with the joy of former years. Now, this is not because of France itself: It is because of that look.

And yet I also know that this will hardly perturb our men of importance—all those clever people who have both feet on the ground and judge the greatness of a nation by the size of its profits. Perhaps they will even take advantage of what I have just confessed in order to boast: '*Our* love does not give way for so little!' They will even give me lessons in patriotism. What shall I answer them? They are stronger than I: they will shut my mouth.

> Vercors, *La Marche à l'étoile*

THE "ANTI" HAS ITS ROOTS EVERYWHERE

One has to admit it: The roots of anti-Semitism are everywhere. There is no area shielded from their pernicious presence. The conspiracy of the Jewish International is no more than a myth, but the complicity of all shades of the Anti-Jewish International is a reality. The Protocols of the Elders of Zion were not written by the Elders of Zion, but all the Anti-elders of Zion discover in their new Bible words and phrases which they make their own.

These Protocols came into existence in Czarist Russia, in the dark night of the pogroms. One can trace the beginning of that night to as far back as the massacre of the Polish Jews by Chmielniki's cossacks in 1648. The midnight of the pogroms were the mounting waves between the pogrom of Elizabethgrad in 1881 and that of Kichinev in 1903. The dawn was slow in coming: The persecution of the Jews in Soviet Russia by Stalin, Krushchev, and Brezhnev continued that of the Czars. These rough blows of the "anti" provoked reactions in the Jewish consciousness which were as sharp and as overwhelming in Eastern Europe as those which the Dreyfus Affair and the rise of Nazism provoked in the West.

One century after Heine, another Jewish visionary was needed in order to discern the *universal* and not necessarily Germanic irrationalism of anti-Semitism. Writing, like Heine, in German on non-German soil, Franz Kafka, like Heine, knew the German sources of the "anti," but one of the keys of his gigantic mythology was the reduction of anti-Semitism to the *per se* of the absurd. Do not look for any logic in the situation of the heroes of Kafka, if not that their situation derives from the anti-logic of the "anti." Are human beings transformed into vermin? Into what can the "anti" transform the Jew if not into the ashes of crematory ovens, into cakes of soap, into miserable living corpses and guinea pigs eaten away by vermin under the vigilant eye of the Professor carrying out his scientific experiments? Why does the hunted animal dig a hole in order to defend itself against an enemy which it will never see and which will never come, but which causes such anxiety to weigh upon the animal that the animal dies of fear in the barricades of its den? Why, if not that the hunted animal represents the Jew in his hunted existence who dies of anxiety even before one kills him? Why does the penitential colony represent a refined and sadistic form of torture if it is not that this concentration camp is the only kind to which the Jew cornered by the "anti" deserves to be sent? Why does the land surveyor find no way to communicate with the Castle, if it is not because the term "common" is erased from the existential terminology of the Jew, around whom the "anti" erected barricades which hemmed him in on every side? Why is K accused without ever discovering what he is accused of, and why does he die of that accusation, if not that K's trial is the trial of the Jew, accused of the crime of existing?

Why? Why? It is we, the readers, who put the question. Kafka never raises it. In his work, it is self-evident that the "anti" knows no other law than that of the absurd. The absurd knows the answer no more than it knows the question. It is in the absolute of the nonsensical that Kafka sees the only sense of the aggression against the Jew by the "anti."

THE INCARNATION OF THE ABSURD IN HISTORY

Franz Kafka only spilled ink. History spilled blood.

In the work of Franz Kafka, a few individuals were eliminated, and, even then, only in the imagination. In the reality, of which Kafka sketched out a kind of anticipatory vision, six million Jews were eliminated—killed simply because they were Jews. In the period previous to this massacre, another Jewish writer, Stefan Zweig, also writing in German like Heine and Kafka, and like them, living in Europe as a whole rather than in the area of purely Germanic culture, drew up the balance sheet of a world which was disintegrating before his very eyes and with which he too was to disappear into an irrecoverable Yesterday. One should re-read these pages of his *World of Yesterday*. Everything that we have said so far is restated here in a synthesis forged directly out of the tragic experience of a Jew who in 1940 was condemned for the crime of existing.

> . . . What was most tragic in this Jewish tragedy of the twentieth century was that those who suffered it knew that it was pointless and that they were guiltless. . . . To integrate themselves and become articulated with the people with whom they lived, to dissolve themselves in the common life, was the purpose for which they strove impatiently for the sake of peace from persecution, rest on the eternal flight . . .

> Only now, since they were swept up like dirt in the streets and heaped together, the bankers from their Berlin palaces and sextons from the synagogues of Orthodox congregations, the philosophy professors from Paris and Romanian cabbies, the undertaker's helpers and Nobel prize winners, the concert singers and hired mourners, the authors and distillers, the haves and the have-nots, the great and the small, the devout and the liberals, the usurers and the sages, the Zionists and the assimilated, the Ashkenazim and the Sephardim, the just and the unjust besides which the confused horde who thought that they had long since eluded the curse, the baptized and the semi-Jews—only now, for the first time in hundreds of years, the Jews were forced into a community of interest to which they had long since ceased to be sensitive, the ever-recurring—since Egypt—community of expulsion.

> But why this fate for them and always for them alone? What was the reason, the sense, the aim of this senseless persecution? . . . None could answer. Even Freud, the clearest-seeing mind of this time, with whom I often talked in those days, was baffled and could make no sense out of the nonsense. . . .

3

The "Meta" and Its Morphoses

AND YET, PERHAPS

If Stefan Zweig's text had ended on this note of absolute meaninglessness, my book would also have run the risk of having to end on this absolute. I would then have had to have devoted it not to those who refashioned their souls, but to those among the Jews whose soul was unfashioned by the "anti"—a complete and absolute defeat. Where the clearest-seeing mind of our time—yes, where Freud, even Freud could find no path—who could have found even a symbol, even a sign, even a figment of a path?

To all appearances, meaninglessness had triumphed. Freud, in fact, had died in London in despair a few months before Zweig had written this text, and Zweig himself chose death in the impasse of absurdity in Rio de Janeiro in 1942.

And yet here is the Jewish rebound, looming up from the depths of the abyss. The text of Stefan Zweig rebounds in a phrase—a single one. It is equivalent to a revolution:

> But perhaps the ultimate significance of Judaism may be that through its mysterious survival it constitutes a reiteration of Job's eternal cry to God, so that it may not be quite forgotten on earth.

Everything takes place upon earth, in the horizontal dimension, and yet a small aperture suddenly appears in the walls of Kafka's castle—the aperture of "perhaps." I, too, have written a book in which I have tried to bring a glimmer of light into the dark night, a suggestion of word within the silence, and I, too, finished with what I called the "fugue of perhaps." The hypothetical "maybe"—a hostage given up to fortune, a soap bubble floating up to heaven which may get lost and evaporate but which also may be—constitutes the basis from which being can recommence.

Here on earth, it is no longer a question of a man but of Job. Here on earth one no longer has the horizontal pattern of man hunted by man, but the vertical pattern of the Jew harassing God. Thus the enigma of time is electrified by the eternity of a question. There is no longer just the "anti": The "meta" plants itself within it, penetrating to its deepest roots. Would not the "Jewish question" then, posed and solved with such ferocious brutality by the "anti," be simply the point of encounter of the question put by the Jew to God and the question put by God to the Jew? Might not the Jew hunted by man *perhaps* simultaneously be hunted by God?

SOME FOUL BLOWS ARE STROKES FROM THE HEAVENS

God is less patient than man. The Eternal Being is less slow moving than ephemeral beings. Involved in time, the human creature gropes about, advances, retreats, loses his way, drops off to sleep. So many routes cross his topography that he can arrange for halts here and there, today or tomorrow, or in the "afterwards," the other, in the alibi or in alienation.

But the Creator compresses infinity into the single instant. Clouds, to be sure, sometimes gather as a precursory sign, but usually the storm breaks within the arc of the blue sky. Whatever the case—whether sensed as a message or seen as a foul blow—the divine irruption acts like thunder. It is a stroke from the heavens. It is flashing. It is incandescent.

Thus, the creature has to carry the burden of the "meta" whatever its weight. Metaphors (i.e., bearers of the *meta*) are no longer merely images. The symbol is embodied in living experience.

That is the extreme situation of the Jew found again by God. From within his alienation, the Jew, in encountering the Living God, is restituted to himself. Franz Rosenzweig's *teshuva* was a sudden flash whose understanding was given to only two beings: God and the *ba'al teshuva*, or that, at any rate, was the case in the Berlin Synagogue on the Day of Atonement, 1913. Rosenzweig subsequently brought the experience under control and patiently allowed it to work itself out, but on October 11, 1913, the impatience of God took hold of a Jew and brought him back to himself on the spot. The experience lived by Franz Rosenzweig was a pure meta-phor (carrier of the "meta," as we have said) without any admixture of the "anti." It was a religious shock, in which religion regained its initial significance as a link (Latin, *religio*, bond)—a connection between two beings which until that precise moment had been separated by an abyss.

But in order to throw a bridge over this abyss, God also has more dilatory methods. The rainbow of His Covenant has numerous strings. Some are of so great a sensitivity that they have only to vibrate in order to provoke in response the vibrations of the benumbed Jewish heart.

THE FASCINATION OF THE SHEMA

The fascinations of the "meta" are like magnets, and the magnetic field of the Jewish "meta" is a broad one.

The first of these magnets is childhood: First of all, no doubt, because that is where one's roots lie (this is not only true for the Jew but for everyone), and also because childhood is associated with innocence. Whoever from some corner of his mature existence looks back upon his childhood will receive a definite impression of "not yet." An escape into childhood is a fleeting recuperation of the past—of a virgin past, starting out from which the pages of life could have been written differently.

Six Hebrew words accompany the Jew from the cradle to the grave. They are the first which he learns to stammer and the last which he says or hears on his deathbed:

"Shema Israel, Adonai Elohenu, Adonai Ehad."
"Hear, O Israel, the Lord is our God, the Lord is One."
(Deuteronomy 6:4)

One day the German-Jewish literary critic Alfred Kerr, after a radiant voyage in Eretz Israel, wanted to convey a feeling of vertigo, of vertiginous ascension. He was unable to find the words. He therefore substituted six dashes

— — — — — —

as a sort of cryptic message which his Jewish readers were immediately able to decipher. They represented the six words of the Shema.

It is the Shema with which the lost Jew is confronted. "Hear!" This is an interjection thrown out across the two sides of an abyss above which is played out the ambiguous fate of the Jew: his choice between acceptance and rejection, between presence and desertion. In the theology of the Shema, the *logos* of God fluctuates between monologue and dialogue. The Jew is now called, summoned into the area created by the exclamation, "Hear O Israel!" and asks himself: "Why do I, a son of Israel, not listen?"

The "ancient prayer neglected for so many years," "the forgotten faith" (Arnold Schönberg) hidden in these six unique words returns like a haunting refrain. Schönberg attached it to the conclusion of his rendering of the narrative of the survivor of the Warsaw Ghetto in connection with the theme of martyrdom. Heine included it in his Rabbi of Bacharach, set on the banks of the Rhine in the times of the Crusades. Edmond Fleg used it as the title of his Jewish *Légende des siècles*. André Spire made it the banner of his Jewish "Marseillaise": "Hear, O Israel, to arms!" Karl Wolfskehl saw it as the seal of Messianic redemption: "Earth, heaven—a single unified Shema,'' and Benjamin Fondane made it the tragic theme of his return to God, the cry of his *teshuva:* ''In a tongue I have forgot, but remember in Thy fearful nights of wrath . . . in the immaculate center of the ode . . . Adonai Elohenu, Adonai Ehod! . . .

THE SEARCH FOR AN ADDITIONAL SOUL

Other magnets are the halting places on the Jewish paths of time, halting places missed by the alienated Jew who suffered from having to run without stopping when the ''meta'' had created the havens of the Sabbath, Passover, and Yom Kippur where he could have refreshed himself.

No one has ever celebrated the poetry and charm of both the Sabbath and of Passover Night with more sentiment and truth than Heinrich Heine, and yet Heine in his youth hardly knew the Sabbath or the Seder, but the fact is that for the *ba'al teshuva* these two special times are not necessarily connected with his personal memories. Here, the ''meta'' works through the collective memory. The emotional charge of the Sabbath and the Seder is carried in an uninterrupted chain across the generations. Sometimes one has to go back to one's forefathers lost in the mists of time in order to discover that the Sabbath and the Seder were not mirages but events which were actually experienced. Always, however, the transmission was to some degree accompanied by a certain twinge of regret, and all those who had that experience recognized that it was in that feeling of regret that was to be found the source of the sense of pain and frustration in their own lives. One single Sabbath could repair the broken fragments of the Jewish soul, restore to the wandering Jew his blessed halting place in the continuity of time, transfigure the lousy tramp into a Prince Charming and bestow on him the ''additional soul'' which Jewish tradition promises the observer of the Sabbath. One single Sabbath observed by all the Jews, says the Midrash, could bring the Messiah.

When everyone goes off in search of some vague and inaccessible ''over there,'' the Sabbath provides the security of the eternal and immutable ''here'':

> Only one's forefathers (what to do?) remained in
> a land
> Which wasn't theirs—and celebrated
> Saturday.

> Benjamin Fondane, 1944

When the hateful society of the ''anti'' infects the Jew with the ''mind of a dog,'' every seven days Princess Sabbath touches the Jew with her magic wand, and lo and behold, for twenty-four hours he again becomes a man and more than a man—a metaphor of human light as radiant as invincible hope (Heinrich Heine 1851, Ernst Bloch 1951).

LIVING A QUESTION

A single Seder with its initial question: "Why is this night different from all other nights?" could lay hold of a Jew in his unalterable otherness and force him to understand—and to relate—in which way he, a man like all other men, is nevertheless distinct from all other men. The "rude awakening" produced by the Seder which Heine spoke about was not due to the cadence of a familiar traditional melody but the surging up in front of the Jew of a destiny which he thought he was rid of and which each Seder Night comes back to him with a fascinating power.

For that reason Bernard Lazare began his *Fumier de Job* with the dramatic scenario of the Seder:

> . . . It is Passover evening, the Seder ceremony performed at a friend's or at a relative's. They are all there, drawn by various motives (the poor man, the old man, the proletarian, each unknown to the other, have taken their places at table, having been brought back from the synagogue by the master of the house who is faithful to custom). The narrative begins, interrupted by a noise in the street, shouts of 'Death to the Jews!' There are various reactions from the people present—the eternal persecution (a reminder of former times), the eternal exodus, stories of bygone days, the eternal people, the solutions already offered; the necessity of understanding and knowing the soul of the Jewish people (the children of the Haggada) . . .

THE "META" IN ITS HUMAN
RELATIONSHIP: THOU ART MY PEOPLE

Here the "meta" agrees to take on apparently horizontal forms. What the *ba'al teshuva* seeks in the Sabbath and the Seder is not so much to encounter God as to go back to the infancy of the people and to find one's place once more in the chain of lived and experienced history—a history which was able to resist the temptations of otherness and to safeguard its essential nature, the simplicity of its comprehensive Jewish identity.

The myth of Emancipation had underlying it the principle of Clermont-Tonnerre's dictum: "Everything to the Jew as an individual, nothing to the Jews as a nation." It was a rule that was intended to be tolerant, but it was cynical and mutilating. The Jew, adopting it, and happy, by this means, to acquire his liberty, lived like a solitary tree, fearing to admit his solidarity with the other trees of the forest. Solidarity came into being as soon as the blows of the axe against one solitary tree caused the whole forest to tremble. That was the Dreyfus Affair.

All of a sudden, certain Jews, stripped of their Jewishness as individuals, regained it through the discovery of the people to which they belonged. Heinrich Heine, Bernard Lazare, and Franz Rosenzweig awoke to Judaism—or else became more aware of it through contact with the Jewish people, seen first with curiosity, then with love, and then finally with a burning desire to be adopted by it.

Many were the ingrained mythical prejudices about the people which had to be discarded. One had to become conscious of the fact that they existed in flesh and blood, living, teeming in thousands and millions. Thousands and millions? No, these were not Jews like the Rothschilds. This was a poor people: proletarians, workers, artisans, tramps, but of a nobility of soul which was greater than that of the barons and bankers. It was a wretched people, but happy in their rites, their prayers, their customs, their longings. A people for whom Judaism was not a misfortune but a privilege, or, rather, something still more precious than a privilege: It was accepted with a natural simplicity as self-evident because it had been given by God.

Thus the veil of ignorance came to be lifted. Heinrich Heine, Bernard Lazare, and Franz Rosenzweig had to make voyages to Central and Eastern Europe before they were able to divest themselves of the myth of two unequal worlds: the myth of the educated Jews of Western Europe and the filthy Jews of the East—the *Polacks*, the *Ostjuden*.

In a page by Heinrich Heine on the Jews of Poland, written in 1822, one passes from contempt to pity, and then from pity to envy. The text is so full of flavor that it would lose its taste by being translated. I can only attempt a rough paraphrase. What is fascinating about these Jews, he said, is their wholeness: They are Jews, and that is that. The Western Jew is constricted by ridiculous and vain attempts to appear "like the others." His civil status is a jumble of regulations, of instructions, of edicts of tolerance, of half-tolerance, of quarter-tolerance: He carries it like a fool's motley. Despite appearances, it is not the *streimel*, the Polak's fur hat which is ridiculous, for it is a Jewish hat, worn by a Jew. On the other hand, the top hat or felt hat of the Western Jew makes him into a clown. He would like to be regarded as a human being, but all he succeeds in "humanizing" is his headgear. His body, meanwhile, remains Jewish, and that makes a grotesque combination, while the Polish Jew is authentically all of a piece.

Later, at the end of the nineteenth century and the beginning of the twentieth, it was Bernard Lazare who found himself by discovering the Jews of Eastern Europe. In *Les cahiers de la Quinzaine* he sought to rehabilitate the Jews of Romania—no, he shouted their rehabilitation—with as prophetic an indignation as that of his cry for the rehabilitation of Dreyfus.

In *Le Fumier de Job* he waxed lyrical in describing the poetry of Hasidic life:

> Life in the synagogue of the Hasidim.
> One is there at all hours of the day, especially on Friday afternoons and Saturdays. One prays there, one sings there, one sleeps there at night when one has no shelter. One sleeps there in the daytime. One eats there on Saturday evening after the study of the Law. One commentates it, one teaches it. It is the Hasid's universe: It is there that he forgets his wretchedness. It is there that, through a frantic sensual mysticism, he escapes reality. One should see them there on Saturday evenings after prayers, at about seven-thirty in the month of May. They sit in the synagogue around a table, and they eat. Each one brings with him a little *halles* (challah bread) and they drink liquor. Then, when they have eaten, the songs begin in the growing twilight. Before night falls, they sing joyful songs—and tomorrow they will have nothing to eat.

When the vicissitudes of war brought Franz Rosenzweig to the Warsaw Ghetto in May 1918 (nearly a century after Heine!), it was an experience of discovery that produced a deep and lasting trauma. Theological arguments, increasingly based on the practical experiences which were becoming more and more common owing to the military expeditions outside Germany, had prepared Rosenzweig to rid himself of the superiority-complex of the Western Jew. In 1916, he had written to his parents that the "Jewish question" did not only concern the Jews of the East, and, contrary to what the German Jews, convinced that their Judaism would no longer cause any problem, believed, "there is only a Jewish problem as such." And, that same year, in his correspondence with Eugen Rosenstock, he had attempted to demonstrate the oneness of the Jewish destiny and the universal relevance of the questions of existence, of assimilation, and of the threat of anti-Semitism which confront the Jew, whether of the West or of the East.

The festival of Passover 1917, when he was in the Balkans, gave him the opportunity of observing the Sephardic Jews of Macedonia and appreciating their traits of energy. It was there that, for the first time, a schoolboy (with whom he had conversed in French) had seemed to him a representative of the whole Jewish people. Previously, only old people had seemed to him to possess this quality, to such a degree had Judaism been for him a senile phenomenon, a tradition of the past in no way associated with youthfulness or the future. Above all, on this visit, he had re-established a truth which had also been smothered by a century in which the whole weight of Jewish history had been concentrated on Europe: the unity of the Ashkenazim and the Sephardim. "Anyone who says the Sephardim are a different race from us is a liar. They have had a different fate . . . ''

The first Sabbath in the Jewish Quarter in Warsaw produced a psychological upheaval in Rosenzweig. It was no longer a matter of unity or equality: What Rosenzweig found was a Judaism radically different from that of Western Europe, and radically different, also, from the Western European Jews' idea of Eastern European Judaism. He found a Judaism which he instinctively felt to be the only one worthy of the name, the only one to contain the true Jewish values, a Judaism compared to which German Judaism appeared to be a grotesque or even tragic falsification. A series of letters to his mother (his father had died a few weeks earlier, and this period of mourning lent itself to deep reflections) gave an account of the overwhelming quality of Rosenzweig's experience. His explorations were hesitant and advanced by stages from the external characteristics—the character of the Jewish quarter, the costumes, the language—to the inner realities: religious beliefs, liturgical customs, the system of primary and higher education. In each of these stages, however, he experienced the same stupefied amazement. The legend of the filthy, miserable, uneducated, crafty Polish Jew crumbled point by point. It had been carefully sustained by the Western Jews either out of ignorance or else out of the need to find a scapegoat for their own misconceptions. Whatever the case, the Warsaw Jew discovered by Rosenzweig was clean, dignified, cultured, honest—qualities which stood out very clearly in their practical application. The caftans, the gowns, and the skullcaps were not only clean and well kept: They were superlatively beautiful—*wunderschön*. The deportment of the Jews in the street, in the synagogue, in the theater was not only dignified, it had something aristocratic about it. The institutions of primary and higher education, devoted almost entirely to the study of Talmud, not only displayed a high cultural level but used pedagogical methods truly adapted to the specific character of the Jewish people. This high intellectual level was to be found also in the Yiddish theater and in the literary use of the Yiddish language, decried by Occidentals as a retrograde jargon. Finally, these Warsaw Jews were not only honest: They were whole. They had no dichotomy, no hypocrisy, no complexes. In the street, they were the same as at home; with non-Jews, the same as among themselves. They were whole Jews, finding in their Judaism their raison d'être.

BEING TAKEN HOLD OF BY THE "META": YOM KIPPUR

Yom Kippur: the day in the Jewish calendar when every Jew is called upon by God to make his soul anew. It is a day on which even the most integrated, the most complete, the most Jewish of Jews returns to zero and becomes a *ba'al teshuva*. It is thus only natural that Yom Kippur should appear in this book as the "meta" of the "meta." Is it not described in tradition as the culmination of the sacred, the Sabbath of Sabbaths?

This vertical culminating quality of Yom Kippur runs through this book from end to end. I already mentioned it in the prologue when I described Franz Rosenzweig's entry into the Berlin synagogue on the eve of Yom Kippur, the eleventh of October, 1913. "From one evening to the next . . . ," "From the first page to the last," "From Kol Nidre to Ne'ila." The Ne'ila in this book will be Kol Nidre.

What one must point out here is that in Yom Kippur as in the Sabbath and the Seder there is also a horizontal dimension. Yom Kippur is a special moment of encounter of the Jew with God. It is also a special moment of encounter of the Jew with all the other Jews, with the community. One of the reasons, precisely, for Franz Rosenzweig's choice of Yom Kippur as the day to enter the synagogue was that his assimilated family was one of those who in the nineteenth century were known as "three-day Jews." They went to synagogue only on three days of the year—the three solemn days—the two days of Rosh Hashana, or the New Year, and, eight days later, Yom Kippur. In the twentieth century their frequentation of the synagogue was reduced to the single day of Yom Kippur, and this single day has become a decisive element in the sociological test of Jewish identity.

Among the thousand gates of synagogues the world over, each one says but a single word: Return. The Jews hear it and return, each one by his own path: Marranos, crypto-Marranos, those who have strayed, those who are faithful, the regular attendants, those who are distant, strangers. From the opening of the gates—Kol Nidre—to their closing—Ne'ila—the synagogues are full to overflowing (they spill over into the streets and into the annexes: rooms, residences, open fields, prisons, death camps, transformed for twenty-four hours into synagogues), in Saragossa, Marrakesh, Bordeaux, Strasbourg, Frankfurt, Berlin, Warsaw, Berdichev, New York, Moscow . . . and, yes, in Auschwitz, each of these places containing in itself a fragment of history into which the individual inserts himself for twenty-four hours like a link in a chain.

Why did I not mention Jerusalem and Tel Aviv in this list of places of importance in Jewish history? It is because the State of Israel as a whole forms one vast synagogue. There are twenty-four hours of total mechanical stoppage: no transport, cars, scooters, trains, airplanes, mass media, nor transistors, nor television. Nothing but prayer, fasting, and meditation in silence.

It is something unique in the world in the twentieth century: The incarnation of the "meta" in the existence of a state. But is not the State of Israel, in its very existence, a meta-state? And surely, the war launched against Israel on Yom Kippur October 6, 1973, was not only horizontal. Was it not a war whose meta-physical, meta-human resonances continue to reverberate through history?

NEXT YEAR IN JERUSALEM . . .
(We Have so Willed, and It Is not a Dream)

The history of Zionism can be written in the horizontal dimension of the "anti," and this, indeed, is how it has often been interpreted: as a movement of nationalism in response to the anti-Semitism of the nineteenth and twentieth centuries. Two "isms" without a vertical. To subscribe to this idea, however, would be to undervalue Zionism. How often does one have to repeat it? Within the "ism" of Zionism, the Zion implants the vertical of the "meta."

If one wants to point to a precise date in the history of Zionism which illustrates the appearance of the "meta," it was the night of August 23, 1903. On the banks of the Rhine, in Basle, at the Sixth Zionist Congress— his last—Theodore Herzl presented the Jews with the offer made to them by the British government of the territory of Uganda. It was a providential offer—in the perspective, at least, of practical, political, unidimensional, horizontal circumstance. The Russian Jews had just been afflicted with the Kichinev pogrom. Other pogroms threatened the miserable fugitives who filled the blocked routes towards the West or Turkish Palestine. The relieved Zionists of Western Europe applauded: At last a haven had opened its doors to the oppressed. But at that point the Russian Zionists got up: those very ones whose parents, brothers, and children were being threatened in Russia. They fought the whole night long—and won the victory—for the "Zionism of Zion." The rejection of Uganda, of a land of refuge, of a land other than the land of Zion created an awareness of the responsibility involved in the choice of the simple word "Zionism."

Zion, which is only a fragment of Jerusalem and the Land of Israel, is a word one can neither play around with, nor play tricks with, nor beat about the bush with. It is the key word of the "meta" of Jewish history. Through Zion, Zionism becomes bi-dimensional. The vertical is interlocked with the horizontal.

Zion is Jerusalem the Irreplaceable. "If I forget thee, O Jerusalem! . . . " On the banks of the rivers of Babylon the Jews discovered the interconnection of Jerusalem and the irreplaceable and, since that time, without interruption or suspension or pause or parenthesis, the Jews have experienced, proclaimed, sung, and cried out that interconnection.

I want no other! Neither in Rome nor in Mecca, nor in Paris, nor in New York, nor in Moscow, nor in Peking. I want no other, and I refuse to replace Jerusalem below, be it dust and ruins, by another Jerusalem, be it Edenic but in heaven.

I want no other! cried the Jews, during the bitter sobbing of the nights and the faint glimmerings of the dawns. I want no other! cried the Jews, each time that on the long road of exile someone proposed another Jerusalem, a sure and comforting resting place, in exchange for the one which, over there on its rock, seemed quite forlorn and could only offer the stones of an aging Wall to which, moreover, they were soon to be forbidden access.

Never, thanks to the irreplaceable Jerusalem, has the Jew been the Wandering Jew of legend. He has always been the Pilgrim of Jerusalem. Never has he found a home, for his longings have made him a perpetual Lover of Zion. The exile is a path: the path of return to Jerusalem.

No computer could ever assess the number of times the words "Zion," "Jerusalem," and "Land of Israel" occur in the texts of the Jewish liturgy, Jewish poetry, and Jewish philosophy, for these texts are pervaded with an insane hope which makes these appeals as innumerable as the sands of the sea, as the stars of the firmament. Divest the Jew of his last vestige of Jewish consciousness and there will still remain in the inviolable depths of his meta-consciousness a phrase as pure as a child's dream, as splendid as a flight of eagles with wings outspread, as moving as the response of the beloved to the voice of the lover, as vibrant with hope as with certitude, and that is: "Next year in Jerusalem."

THE DIALECTICS OF THE "ANTI" AND THE "META"

The "anti" and the "meta" usually work together in conjunction, but with a sufficient difference of intensity to allow the horizontal aspect of the Return to be clearly distinguished from its vertical aspect. What, at any rate, cannot be doubted is that there are Jews who have reacted to the "anti" without being conscious of a "meta": Their return envisages no more than their own selves, their people, and their destiny as Jews in the human adventure. It is we who, in the course of analysis, insert a "meta," a vertical implication, a "finger of God" into something which for them has no conscious connection with the absolute.

Conversely, there are Jews touched by God who have not felt in the divine aggression a presence or reminder or residue of any human aggression. The shock of the "anti" was not any kind of factor before or during the shock of the "meta."

In the birth of the State of Israel, however, there was a perfect simultaneity of the "anti" and the "meta." Without the Dreyfus Affair, without the shock created by the cry "Death to the Jews!," Herzl would not have done *teshuva*. Without the Uganda Affair, however, without the shock created by the cry "Next year in Jerusalem!," the Zionist movement would not have been fully Zionist. Man and God worked together to bring the nineteenth and twentieth centuries from assimilation to Zionism, and to restore unity to the split condition of the modern Jew.

What, we may ask, was the mask taken by God in this decisive encounter? What was the morphosis (form) of this "meta" which illumines all the others and gathers them up within itself?

In order to answer this question, we must turn once again to the testament of Stefan Zweig.

YES, PERHAPS

It is altogether remarkable that Stefan Zweig should have attached his ultimate anchor—the "perhaps" of a meaning to meaninglessness—to the biblical figure of Job. If Freud had still been alive, he might *perhaps* have explained that even suicide can have a meaning. Did it not have one for the stoics, for Albert Camus? It had one for Job's wife also, who offered the suffering Job the chalice of euthanasia: "Bless God and die!" But Job refused this chalice. He did not wish God to take the suffering away from him. What he wanted was to learn from God the meaning of his ordeal. Stefan Zweig's suicide was not a Jewish act. It was the very opposite, but the fact remains that at a certain moment Stefan Zweig asked himself if a way did not nevertheless exist to get out of the impasse, and if that way had not left its trace in the Bible.

It is altogether remarkable that Freud, before dying, should have expressed his regret at having written *Moses and Monotheism* during the years when Nazism was rising to power. His book could only add one more weapon to the arsenal of the "anti," and it proved to be a fearful one. Another Zweig, the novelist Arnold Zweig, a Zionist and communist Jew, a disciple of Freud, had begged his Master not to write this *Moses*, and, having written it, not to publish it. Freud, however, went ahead. Now exiled, persecuted, cornered in his Jewish condition, he recognized that he had sinned. Here this word "sin," which had no meaning in Freud's teaching, was suddenly full to overflowing with vertical content because it was a sin against the Bible. The "meta," despite everything, breaks through the strata of the physical consciousness and rends them through a metaphysical aggression which in the Bible is at the same time a wounding and a healing. This is the struggle of Jacob with the angel (Genesis 32).

It is altogether remarkable that Franz Kafka also discovered the sole ray of light in his universe of the absurd in the Bible. "I opened the Bible," he noted in his diary for September 16, 1915. "The unjust judges (the Book of Job). Here, then, my own opinion is confirmed, or rather the opinion that I have found already formed in me hitherto . . . "

Franz Rosenzweig, who read Kafka only at a late stage, was also struck with the similarity of Kafka's themes with those of the Bible. "The people who wrote the Bible," he said, "apparently had the same idea of God as Franz Kafka. I have never read a book which reminded me so much of the Bible as his story *The Castle* . . . "

Was not Heine's decision to read the Bible also significant? And Bernard Lazare's switch from a secular idiom to the writing of *Le Fumier de Job* (Job's Dunghill)? Charles Péguy, who better than anyone else understood Lazare's development, had no doubt about the matter at all. For Péguy, the Bernard Lazare of the Dreyfus Affair was not a lawyer, a propagandist, or pamphleteer: He was a "prophet," he said, switching to biblical language. "This atheist," he said, "was brimming over with the Word of God"—a phrase which Péguy wrote long before the pages of *Le Fumier de Job,* which Péguy never read, were retrieved from the drawers in which Lazare had buried them before he died.

The pogrom at Kichinev traumatized the Russian Jews at the time when the Dreyfus Affair was dying down in the West. In order to give vent to his frustration at a tragic situation where the Jewish people and their God were both gripped in one and the same revolting passivity, the poet Haim Nahman Bialik took from the Bible the complex theme of the "Dead of the Desert." The desert, however, is nothing other than an interval of time and space intermediate between an Exodus and an Entry into a Promised Land. A time and a space of wandering, cut adrift from one's moorings, with one's anchor not yet cast upon a Land which still remains to be discovered.

Le'an? Whither? cried the Russian Jew beneath the axe of the pogroms. *Le'an?* Whither? cried the German Jew beneath the blade of the swastika. *Le'an?* cries the Jew everywhere, transfixed by an alienation which proves to be illusory, dangerous, fatal.

Here, once again, it was the Bible that provided the hunted Jew with his themes. Exodus, Exodus, Exodus. . . . Karl Wolfskehl and Benjamin Fondane inscribed the word, the thing, and the experience in poems which were cries from the Bible.

MAYBE THE MESSIAH

Is the Exodus a leap into the unknown, or else, over there, at the end of the road, on the horizon, is it the goal? The line of the horizon vanishes as one approaches it, but the Jew knows that even if the horizon vanishes, in its vanishing it turns towards a vertical position. This point of turning towards the vertical is the "may be" of the Messiah. It is unreal. That is why it has to be created. Yet it is real because it is promised in the very act which creates it. It is the paradox of a mirage which awaits, in order to be, he who labors in order that it *should* be. This is the dividing line between the Christian Messiah and Jewish Messianism. It is the Messianic vocation of each Jew in himself. The Messianic "meta" awaits the readiness and the action of the Jewish child-prophet.

"What must I do to be Jewish? What must I do? What must I do? Then there was a great silence. Then, a murmur from very far away.

"Bring him over here!"

Then there was a great light and, against that light, a great cross. And, on that cross, Jesus, bleeding, agonizing. And he said:

"The Messiah of peace, the Messiah of justice, he whom I wished to be, he whom I was not—make him come!"

Edmond Fleg

When I was a child, our teacher told us that the Messiah was waiting at the gates of Rome. I ran home and impatiently asked my grandfather: 'Then, whom is he waiting for?' And grandfather answered: 'He's waiting for you!'

Martin Buber

Moses Hess was no longer a child when the Messianic "meta" led him, between 1840 and 1862, from Karl Marx to Rabbi Zvi Hirsch Kalischer. Hess was not only Marx's comrade but his teacher: It was with Moses Hess that Marx and Engels learned the elements of dialectical, revolutionary, and utopian socialism. This was before the revolution of 1848. Exiled in France, Hess now became enthusiastic about movements of national liberation, especially the Italian one, but when he came to write his great work *Rome and Jerusalem* in 1862, he asked for more than the fulfillment of the right of the Jewish people *also* to create its own state on its own soil, Palestine. In the opinion of Hess, that state would have to be inspired by the socialism of Moses. It should and could find its guiding principles in Jewish Messianism: those principles which Rabbi Kalischer had set out in Hebrew in his booklet *Derishat Tzion*. It was with a translation into German of that vertical appeal of the "meta" that Moses Hess concluded the dialectical analysis which made him a precursor of Herzl's Zionism.

Among the Zionists who made their existence in the Jewish National Home which subsequently became the State of Israel, I mentioned, in the initial section of this book, Aaron Abraham Kabak and the Nazir of Jerusalem.

One burning night was sufficient to bring them back from the world of European culture to the "yoke," accepted in joy, of the Jewish Torah and mitzvot, but what drew them to this process of transfiguration was the Messianic thrust of the Law and of observance.

When Kabak was still a secular socialist and freethinker, as Moses Hess also was for a long period, he wrote a story entitled "The Obstinate One" about a young Jew who died of wanting to be the Messiah—that same wish to be the Messiah that, in another context, one finds in Edmond Fleg and Martin Buber. Kabak's *teshuva* sprang out of his desire to implant this "wishing to become" into life. It is also remarkable that the burning night which made the freethinker Kabak into a believer and an observer of the Torah was flanked by two literary masterpieces. One was consecrated to Shlomo Molko, a Jew who thought he was the Messiah and died a martyr's death, burnt at the stake by the Inquisition at Mantua in 1532, and the other, written by Kabak just after his return to full-scale Judaism, was a novel about Jesus of Nazareth. Thus Kabak, a writer of genius, transferred onto two eminent Jewish figures who had "died of wanting to be the Messiah" the obsession of his youth. Now, through his *teshuva*, he helped, through each of his acts of observance, to bring the coming of the Messiah to pass.

Even more than Kabak, Rav Hanazir was a co-worker with the Messiah. He continued the mystical dream of his Master, Rav Kook, whose works he published: so many seeds sown into the Land of Israel in view of a Messianic garnering. In each stage in the life of the State of Israel he heard the Messiah's footsteps: in its birth in 1948, and in the reunification of Jerusalem in 1967. It was his son-in-law, a chaplain and parachutist in the Israeli army, who sounded the shofar at the recapture of the Western Wall. At the age of eighty, a few weeks before the Yom Kippur War, which he did not live to see, Rav Hanazir published a book in which he condensed a lifetime of philosophical, political, and mystical reflections. The writers he had abandoned after that burning night of 1915 were to be found here, bearers, also, of a message which, starting from Israel, embraces the whole of humanity. Socrates, Plato, Descartes, Kant, Hegel, and Schopenhauer dance a harmonious round hand in hand with Philo, Rabbi Akiva, Maimonides, Moshe Chaim Luzatto, Mendelssohn, and Rav Kook. The "meta" of Jewish Messianism surprised them in a redemptive upsurge which sprang from the origins. *The Voice of Prophecy* by Rav Hanazir of Jerusalem ended with a few verses from a poem by Rav Kook. The "meta" of the Messiah has its source in the Book of Beginnings (Genesis):

From the source of prophecy behold we are called,
From the Spirit of the Messiah blow towards us
  the currents which assail us
Standing upright before this new life,
A return towards the beginning!

In the beginning there was light (first day): a full light which was
shattered following the act of creation in order to accomodate the darkness.
But this initial light was scattered in the cosmos in a thousand sparks which
would be lost without the Righteous and the *ba'al teshuva*. *Or zarua la-
tsaddik:* "Light is sown for the Righteous." It is also sown for the man who
comes back to it, the *ba'al teshuva* who takes it in both his hands and
steeps himself in it body and soul, and with it follows the path which leads
from the place where it was lost to the place where it regains its full, initial
identity.

Part Two

THE SITUATION OF BIBLICAL MAN

" . . . Only the Bible sees."

Franz Kafka

4

The Ontological Psychodrama

RUPTURE AND CONTINUITY

In the beginning was the rupture (second day).

The Christian reading of the Bible has accustomed us for nearly two millennia to load this rupture with heavy ethical connotations: fall, sin, transgression—all of it *original*—so as to bring out the fundamental fact that before order was created, there was disorder. It was with disorder that the history of man began.

Much nearer to us, there is the psychoanalytical reading of the Bible. There is the rupture of the umbilical chord between the creator and the creature with all the sexual connotations automatically suggested by the navel where everything goes awry before it even gets going.

Nearer to us still, there is the structural reading: the disjunction of the conjunction, the misstatement of the statement, the hyphen which dismembers words even while connecting them up, disinformation of the form. Morphosis (dreamlike state), mort-phosis (deathlike state), the death of logics in morphologics, the eternal cemetery of living words.

In this book, we renew acquaintance with a reading nearly six thousand years old: the Jewish reading. It has these special qualities:

1. It came into existence at the same time as the Scriptures and it has, therefore, a contemporaneity with their birth not possessed by later readings.

2. It is contemporary with those who possess this particular tradition at the present day: the Jews.

It is thus original like the others, but at the same time actual, and represents a faultless, uninterrupted continuity between the distant past and this very day.

The Jewish reading contains within itself the paradox of a rupture which endures and a duration which is constantly disrupted. The writer of this book, being Jewish, is situated at the heart of this paradox, but it is also a general human paradox since, according to my reading, the first person to be subject, like myself, to this paradox was Adam, man.

THE DIALOGUE OF THE COVENANT

In the beginning was the rupture, and then there came a longing for the original unity. In the end, in the form of a residue whose name is the promise and whose geometrical shape is the horizon, that original unity is to be recreated. Between these two ends, there is the tightrope of the Covenant: in Hebrew, *Brit*.

At the outset of human history, in the womb of time, when the extraordinary work was being undertaken which was to give birth to the world, the Covenant was established, but this involved a challenge whose echo is to be heard in the term *na'asei* ("let us") which occurs so surprisingly in the first chapter of Genesis as a solemn introduction to the appearance of man.

If the plural form of this imperative "Let us make man!" is itself a theological scandal since it offends the strict monotheism of the Torah, an equally scandalous enigma is posed by the collective form of this verb. What need is reflected by this deliberation, this hesitation of God before creating man? What a contrast between the sovereign facility with which the divine Word had previously caused things to spring up out of nothing, and the encouragement with which God now has to provide himself, as if His Word were suddenly lacking in triumphant energy, as if the creator's confidence in Himself were shaken! What is God frightened of in getting down to work at once? What are His scruples? Perhaps this collective form is not the sign of a monologue but the expression of a dialogue. In that case, to whom is God addressing Himself in order to obtain some advice, some help, some agreement, in order to overcome some resistance or get some cooperation? Is it the angels, the earth, the whole universe, or man, whose creation could not be brought to the point of realization unless he himself gave his agreement?

The underlying meaning of these questions is that a challenge had been hurled by God at the insurmountable abyss which separated the creator from the creature, the offerant from the recipient. A deep, hidden, irreducible tension opposed them, set them at a distance from one another, and placed them in positions of mutual confrontation. It was this tension, precisely, which was the object of this collective *na'asei* which was intended to overcome it all at once and to forge an unbreakable agreement between two "sides" whose guiding principle was contestation and disaccord. *Na'asei* was a risk taken by God through which the relationship between God and man was instituted, given a basis, continued, and tested.

It is at the very heart of this wager that the Jewish *teshuva* is situated. The meaning of this word cannot be rendered by any similar notion, and certainly not by the Christian *metanoia*. Franz Rosenzweig noted this fact in the sentence which served as an introductory quotation to this book, a sentence taken from one of his letters to his baptismal sponsor, his cousin Rudolf Ehrenberg, in the days following the memorable Yom Kippur of 1913 in Berlin. The Jews we are speaking about in this book undoubtedly made their souls anew, but they did so by retracing their route: Footsteps led them back to God. These footsteps, however, were never solitary: the rhythm which accompanied them was the same as that which brought God back to these Jews, meeting them at the point of the Covenant which was now nearer to God, now nearer to the Jews, a point eternally linked to the fleeting instant when the *na'asei,* the original "Let us" bound, if only in a wager, God to man and man to God. When that wager was transmuted into history, then drama came into being.

For in the labyrinth of history—a history which is narrated to us in the Bible in the successive stages of a Genesis and an Exodus—man and God get lost. They lose one another, but first of all they lose themselves. They call out, but, often, neither one nor the other hears the call, and often, when they do hear it, neither one nor the other understands the message, and even when they do imagine that they understand it, they misjudge its meaning; and finally, when they do come to grips with one another, they feign the distance of ignorance: "God? Who is he?" "Man? Never heard of him!" And the game goes back to where it began: the ninth verse of the third chapter of Genesis.

THE ONTOLOGY OF THE MASK

In this verse, Adam's being curls up within the four cubits of his ego: He hides. He has won the wager of the rupture. There were a thousand ways he could have broken the Covenant, and his descendants did not fail to utilize them, to squander them, to refurbish them either as temporary existential prescriptions or as well-presented ideologies. One could cite the death of man (Cain), flight (Jonah), the wall of silence (Ezekiel), wisdom (Socrates), suicide (Seneca), dogma (the Churches), anti-dogma (Voltaire), atheism (Feuerbach), positivism (Auguste Comte), revolution (Marx), and the Death of God (Nietzche).

Adam chose life, but a hidden life, away from the eye of God. A life for oneself—a naked life. But in Hebrew, the word *arum*—naked—also means ruse or cunning. It was the first *ruse* in history. Contrary to Hegel, the Bible asserts that it was not the immanent dialectic of history which was responsible for this ruse, but the liberty which the Covenant granted to Adam.

However, God also had His share in the liberty granted by the Covenant. He too was to win the wager of the rupture, but through the paradox of forging a stronger connection than the one that had preceded the rupture. God takes up Adam's challenge by also putting on a mask. He enters into Adam's game, into his ruse. He behaves as if something or someone in the cosmos created by Him could, in a reality as naked as Adam's nakedness, escape His vision. Where are you? *Ayekha?*

Where are you, apple of my eye, cherished creature, Adam whom I modeled with your own assistance, you without whom I am but a fraction of Myself? Where are you? Through what unforgivable absentmindedness did I avert My gaze from you, My hand, My fist, My yoke, that yoke within which I thought we were forever bound, both of us free, but within the impassable limits of the Paradise of our Covenant? Is Hell, then, the other person? Could Sartre be right? Is it our unalterable otherness which has transformed Paradise into an infernal labyrinth in which I cry without an echo, without a response? Where are you, Adam? Where are you?

COMEDY, TRAGEDY . . .

At this point there open up the two henceforth contradictory paths of *teshuva*: the path of the psychodrama whose non-encounter belongs to comedy, and that of the metadrama—the perpetual tragedy of a curtain which can no longer rise because it has fallen from the start.

One has the psychodrama of Adam, his reaction to the tormenting question "Where are you?"—laughter, the victorious sign of liberty.

"What!" laughed Adam, "The creator doesn't know where His creature is?" Like an anxious father he sought the child whom he thought lost, gone astray, dead, torn asunder by wild beasts, suicided perhaps. "Soon," laughed Adam, "God will send after me the police of the Garden, the detectives and the watchdogs! And here am I hidden, perfectly quiet, eternal and naked, with my naked Eve in this corner of Paradise where I am going to remain just like that just for the sake of it, just in order to 'play,' just to see how many times God will pass and re-pass right next to me without finding me!"

It's the human comedy. Suddenly, something went wrong with the comedy. Was God's voice too loud? Was there a hint of menace in it? Was there in the question some kind of bait waiting for its victim? Or was Adam's nakedness divested of everything, even of the ruse and malice which in language are one and the same thing, but in real life do not stop Adam from shivering? Why cannot Adam yet know the nakedness of Eve and her warmth? Why, breaking his alliance with the eternal God, did he also break his alliance with the Eternal Feminine? Why, in renouncing the One (Hebrew *ehad*, numerical value thirteen), did he also destroy love (Hebrew *ahava*, numerical value thirteen)?

Suddenly, Adam was frightened. He hid his face. God's question "Where art thou?" was not an admission of powerlessness: It re-established the equilibrium of the broken alliance (Covenant). God also hid his face. The Hidden Face of God! One would have to pass through all the long drawn-out experience of the Bible, the journeys of the patriarchs, the exile in Egypt, and the crossing of the desert, the settlement in Canaan, the revolt of the psalmists, of Job and the prophets, and, finally, the vision of the prophets, before a ray of light could penetrate the opaque silence, partner of the Hidden Face. But now, at the outset of the drama, just when the curtain apparently ought to have risen, it fell abruptly, and so Adam experienced fear, anxiety, terror, and panic. He was faced with the terrifying possibility of eternal solitude. Will the sun which has set never rise again? Will the moon which has vanished never appear again? Am I condemned to the protracted nightmares of the solitary walker? *My God, my God, why hast Thou forsaken me?* Adam had already forgotten that he had been the first to retreat, and that it was he that had abandoned God. He already absolved himself of all responsibility and blamed God for the weight that was crushing him. Adam was already hatching within him the cry of Cain. The fraternal alliance with God carries within it the risk of fratricide. It's the human tragedy.

THE EXIT

Now, someone who wasn't frightened was Cain. Like his father Adam, he was tracked down with a question of God's : not "Where art thou?" but "Where is thy brother?" He, however, did not hide. He stood upright before God, bold and domineering. To God's question he replied with a counter-question: "Am I my brother's keeper?" (Genesis 4:9).

"My brother's keeper, is it not You, great Caesar, who looks on impassively at my quarrel with Abel as though at the gladiatorial games, and who then dares to call me to account for the murderous gesture which you, precisely, you exclusively could have prevented by ordering the games to be stopped before they turned to tragedy? It's too easy to put the blame on me, and not to admit that you have been implicated together with me from the very moment you created me. Didn't my mother Eve understand that when she declared on weaning me from her breast, "I have gotten a man with God" (Genesis 4:1)? With: yes, together with (Hebrew *et*). Through the power of the Covenant, I am together with You and You are together with me. If you did not want me to annihilate my brother who encroached upon my empire, You had only to prevent my father from knowing my mother. By allowing this knowledge to take place, You mixed up everything! Do

You think You can put everything straight now by condemning me to become a wanderer? Very well, then, I agree to become a wanderer. I turn my back on You, and I leave slamming the door." ("And Cain went out from the presence of God and dwelt in the land of Nod—wandering—on the east of Eden") (Genesis 4:16).

Would Cain, then, be the wandering Prometheus? Does the Bible create, as against the Greek myth of the chained rebel, the myth of the victorious, creative founder-rebel ("And Cain knew his wife; and she conceived, and bore Enoch; and he builded a city, and called the name of the city after the name of his son Enoch") (Genesis 4:17)? Would the wandering represent a more certain rooting, a more certain grafting into eternal values than an acceptance into a Covenant with God? Within the framework of the Covenant, Cain's destiny was to have been a peasant, or, more exactly, according to the precise meaning of the Hebrew expression (4:2), a "slave of the earth." In breaking out of this framework, Cain destroyed his double yoke of servitude. He was no longer either the slave of God nor the slave of the earth. Free at last—fully free, and not only with the ridiculous scrap of free will which God had been ready to concede to him—Cain conceived a new kind of man. God had only created the soil, the *adama;* he would have like man, Adam, to have remained forever a fragment of that *adama.* Cain, however, transmuted the soil into a city: It was the leap from nature to artifice and art. The link between man and his biological origins had now been broken. Those who saw Enoch could no longer distinguish between the son whom Cain had extracted from his body and the city he had built with his hands. Man was henceforth his own master. In transforming the face of the earth, now covered with a vast network of cities, Cain shrouded the face of God. Cain slammed the gates of Heaven in order to find in his wanderings the house of Man.

What Cain had not foreseen in his revolutionary act of defiance, however, was that in the house of Man he was to find, lying in wait on the very threshold for the passerby, the visitor, the stranger, the returner: God!

Thus, Cain's exit in the drama of the Covenant proved to be a false exit, but now we should turn our attention to the finer points of what caused the failure of the exit.

THE FALSE LEGEND OF
THE WANDERING JEW

The ages have handed down to us the legend, so marvelously recalled by Victor Hugo in *La Légende des Siècles,* of a Cain branded with a red-hot iron, pursued by malediction, harried by remorse, blinded by the eye of conscience which, out of the depths of the night, never ceases to stare at him. The Christian centuries have identified this image, at once so marvelous and so hideous, of the fallen and lacerated figure of the eternal wanderer, with the Jew.

One ought not to underestimate the psychopathological significance of this image which is more than merely a pious stereotype. It impregnates human thinking at a sensitive point where it becomes one of the indestructible elements of anti-Semitism.

It haunts certain Jews. For these, the Jewish identity is one and the same thing as wretchedness and wandering. These are the anti-Jewish Jews, the anti-Semitic Jews, the Weiningers, the Trotskys, the Simone Weils, and, long before them, Nicholas Donin and the other Jews of the Middle Ages converted not only to the Church but to the Inquisition. Like Cain, they commit fratricide, kill their brother Jews around them, and, when it is not around them, they kill the brother Jew within themselves. They find the Jewish presence unbearable because it embodies in their vicinity in flesh and blood, or it persists in repeating within their souls and consciences, the idea that "You are Jewish!" And then—Cain multiplied thousands of times—they rise up against the Jew, fraternal mirror image of themselves, and strike him. By means of the word, by means of the pen, by means of the stake. And, if the mirror image still holds, by suicide.

THE TRUE STORY OF THE WANDERING: A RETURN

The authentically Jewish reading gives Cain's false exit a radically different interpretation. To be sure, a number of different possibilities suggest themselves: cunning, hypocrisy, theft, but in the final analysis, the interpretation which wins acceptance is that, unexpected, of joy. It accepts the identification of Cain with the Jew, but it is with the Jew who, after having killed the Jew within himself, becomes Jewish once again.

For, according to this interpretation, Cain, after the verdict has been given, puts a new question to God. When he hears God pronounce the sentence "wandering," Cain, with a wave of proud indignation, rises up: "Is my sin, then, too great to be borne?," he asks (Genesis 4:13). "The heavens and the earth and all their hosts You carry, O majestic Creator—and my own little sin, a humble little earthworm lost in the cosmos, You can't carry, You can't take upon Yourself and forgive?"

This is when God branded Cain with the sign: a sign of protection, a sign of conciliation, a sign of return. " 'And Cain went out . . .' Rabbi Hama said in the name of Rabbi Hanina ben Yitzhak, 'He went out in joy.' " As it is said: "here is your brother who is coming towards you in joy . . . " It was as if Abel had never died, a rediscovery of the broken Tablets of Jewish identity, a reconstitution of the Jewish entity after a fatal and yet reparable breaking apart.

The story could end with this happy ending, but the end, in the Bible, is never simply happy. It transcends happiness through involving unhappiness. Good is only attained through the redemption of evil. Cain gained his happiness only because he created a challenge to the unhappiness of someone else: Adam.

THE SECRET OF TESHUVA

Adam had sinned against no one except God, but that was enough for him to be distraught, disconcerted, torn apart, at a loss. His son Cain who had committed a double crime, sinning against both God and his brother, lived a life which was normal, constructive, edifying. What, then, was the secret of this re-edification, this reconstruction of oneself from one's ruins?

According to the Midrash (Bereshit Rabba 22:28), Adam, saddened, met Cain who was full of joy:

"How did your judgment go?," he asked.
"I did *teshuva* and everything turned out all right."
"Such is the force of *teshuva*," said Adam, beating his forehead, "And I, poor Adam, was not aware of it."
Adam immediately pulled himself up. He began to sing. He sang a song which one day was to enter into the Book of Psalms as number 92: "A song. Psalm for the Sabbath day."

The cause of Adam's suffering was not only having lost Paradise, but not having been able to enter into the Sabbath. Everything related to him had happened during the twelve hours of the sixth day: his birth, his calling by God, his entry into Eden, his union with Eve, his sin, his expulsion— the solitude of the couple banished from Paradise. The psychological and ontological shock was so great that his mind did not retain anything that happened afterwards. The birth of Cain, the birth of Abel, Cain's murder of Abel, Cain's flight: All this was not connected by Adam with any time span. It lasted a day, perhaps, or an hour, or an eternity. The growing up and the fratricide of his first two children were experienced by Adam in a state of schizophrenia, in a diaspora of his being. In order that Adam should be able to find himself again, he had to have the meeting with Cain, whose joy communicated to him a secret—the secret of *teshuva*.

Then, with Adam, body and soul now reasserted themselves. In Adam's disjointed existence one now gets an "again" (Genesis 4:25). Everything had seemed to have been finished: The curtain had apparently fallen on his drama, the lights had gone out. But now the dawn began to dissipate the darkness. Adam regained a soul: The additional soul of the Sabbath which revitalized his own and attuned it to its own Edenic pitch. Adam regained a body: That of Eve, whose otherness, whose complement revived his own and attuned it to its own creative capacities. The original matrix was reconstituted. Adam and Eve again, like Cain, became founders: They founded a family, giving birth to a son, Seth—a "different" son, just as the Psalm for the Sabbath Day was a different psalm, just as the Paradise regained, after their *teshuva*, by Adam and Eve in their radiant union of the Sabbath, was a different Paradise. It was not the former Paradise regained afterwards: it was the seed (*zera aher*, another seed, Genesis 2:25) of the Paradise of after the afterwards, the day following the day after, the Paradise to come—that of the Messiah.

5

The Typological Sociodrama

The life of Moses: a series of situations, each one of which can serve as an archetype of that of the Jew:

> Unlike the Egyptians, Moses did not create his works of art in brick and granite. He built human pyramids, he sculpted human obelisks; he took a poor tribe of shepherds and created out of it a people which, like the Egyptian monuments, was to defy the centuries—a great, eternal, holy people, a people of God, which was to serve as a prototype for all the other peoples, for the whole of humanity. He created Israel!

> Heinrich Heine

WHERE ART THOU, GOD?

The problem of Jewish identity cannot be broached by the question "Who art thou?" The Jew is only concerned with the first question which God puts to Adam in the Book of Genesis: "Where art thou?"

The same applies to the identity of God in Jewish problematics.

"Who is God?" This was the question put by Pharaoh at the time when he was harried by Moses who claimed God's authority for asking that the Jews should be free, that the Jews should "leave," that the Jews should carry out the Exodus.

Genesis and Exodus meet on the crossroads of the "Who?" and the "Where?"

"Who is God? I know not God," Pharaoh tells Moses (Exodus 5:2). "I have never allowed a man to break free of the yoke of my will. I have never seen a man attempting to go against my will. Why the Jews? I do not know God who is demanding their Exodus from me. I don't know the concept God; I don't know the concept Exodus.

"Who is God? I know not God. I consult the list of the divinities of the East and West, of the North and South. It's a complete list: The first divinity is listed as number one. It's an up-to-date list: The first divinity at the present time is me. I carry the heiroglyphic number of the Nile dynasty. I made myself—self-made God—with a little Nile water and a great deal of blood. All the divinities are to be found on this list. None of them has ever spoken nor heard the word Exodus. I don't find the name of God in it, of the God who says 'Let my people go!'' Who is God? I know not God.''

"Pharaoh, if you found God on your list, God would no longer be God. The God of whom I, Moses, am speaking, who spoke to me, Moses, and who asked me to speak to you, Pharaoh—the God who does not communicate with man through miracles, magic, serpents, rods, signs, and plagues, but through the Word. The God whose word is a demand for liberty is the God whose Name cannot figure beside that of any other divinity. It is the unique God who is neither first nor last. Before the first, He was. After the last, He will be. It is the God without a dynasty. He has neither Father nor Son. It is the God without a Name. If you knew His Name, you would not know Him. Even a knowledge of His Being can only be an un-knowing.

"You cannot ask: 'Who is God?' That would be to deny Him. All you can ask is: 'Where is God?'

"And that, precisely, is the question which I, Moses, have been asking ever since the infernal moment when, from my mother's breast, your warders, Pharaoh, watched over my 'exit' in order to drown me in your Nile like a dog. Already, to you, the biological Exodus of a Jew was a crime, but where was God while these crimes were being committed?''

WHERE ART THOU, MOSES?

Moses' Jewish childhood was something which he could have hidden from view, and which, anyway, circumstances hid from him and from those who related it to such a degree that, like certain others—and through an act of deliberate repression—Freud was able to claim that Moses was not Jewish but Egyptian.

But, no! Moses was born Jewish, tragically Jewish. Condemned to be burnt in the gas chambers at Auschwitz, or—in that period—to be drowned in the waters of the Nile. Condemned because he was born Jewish. His crime—to be born Jewish.

Moses was a Jewish child who was rescued. He was one of that handful of wild-eyed Jewish children whom we knew in 1945, a wretched remainder of more than a million Jewish children who were exterminated.

The story of his rescue was complex, it is true, but it would be a diminution of its significance if one were to overlook any of its implications. He was saved by one of the Righteous Gentiles (Bythia, daughter of Pharaoh), and immediately returned to his natural mother. It was thus in his mother's arms, surrounded by his father, his brother Aaron, and his sister Miriam, that Moses, in his cot and when taking his first steps, breathed the Levitical atmosphere of a Jewish home. This initial breath of Jewish oxygen must have had some effect on Moses' conceptual and, perhaps, even more, emotional organism. No doubt, when the child grew (Exodus 2:11), his natural mother brought him back to the Righteous Gentile who had taken him out of the water, had given him his name and had wanted to make him her adoptive son. The long period in which Moses lived in Bythia's Egyptian palace might, in the final analysis, have overlain the previous stratum of Jewish existence, but the fact was that Moses had lived through that stratum from his birth until the time he had reached a certain age. From early on, Moses heard the Sabbath lullaby, intoned by his mother in the hours snatched from grinding slavery. From early on, Moses heard his mother tell him the story of Abraham's sacrifice of Isaac and whisper in his ear: "You too have been rescued like Isaac. . . . Sleep, sleep, little Isaac of mine!" Moses heard without understanding, but with his mind alert, his older brother and sister softly chanting "Next year in Jerusalem," and the Jewish neighbors warning them: "Keep quiet, keep quiet! If the Egyptian overseers and the Jewish kapos should hear us!" In short, he knew fear, hope, Jewish history and poetry, imbibed in the maternal home. Moses put them somewhere in the substrata of his consciousness. In claiming that Moses was born an Egyptian, Freud not only made him the murderer of his father, which in his opinion we all are: He also made him the murderer of his mother. Oedipus did not suffice for Freud to explain Moses: He also had to associate him with Orestes.

Let us continue, for our part, implicating Moses of a sense of Jewish identity, and let us note that this implication is all the more surprising in that according to the mathematical norms of sociology and historical determinism it ought to have come to an abrupt halt and disappeared.

When he lived with Bythia, Moses was an Egyptian prince. Intelligent, he gulped down Egyptian philosophy and won his academic diplomas with distinction. Muscular, he became captain of Pharaoh's celebrated cavalry and gamefully risked his life for his Egyptian homeland on the battlefields of the deserts and the sources of the Nile. He was the very archetype of the assimilated Jew, altogether like the others, no longer finding the slightest Jewish trace in himself. The Bible is uncommunicative about this period, but details abound in the Midrash and the apocryphal books. The Midrash might have said, to use its own terminology, that Moses at that period was the reincarnation of Cain. To be sure, he had not on his own initiative killed the Jew within himself. Quite simply, the Jew within him had died a natural death. For Moses, the Jewish brother had ceased to exist.

The sense of Jewish kinship was extinguished, and, together with that, the continuity of Jewish history.

The writers of the Midrash, however, having read the Bible to the end, found that they were obliged to come to the conclusion that Moses was not to be identified with Cain but with Abel.

THE EXODUS OF THE JEW
TOWARD HIMSELF

Suddenly, violently, without our knowing why, shattering the norms of sociology and history, the awakening of the Jewish consciousness took place in Moses—an awakening which the Bible summarized in a few memorable words: "When Moses was grown, he went out unto his brethren" (Exodus 2:1). It was an identification with Abel of someone whom one had thought to be Cain: After having been extirpated, the kinship was restored. This "going out" is all-important. It is the Exodus par excellence—of the Jew towards himself. It is Return, *teshuva*. In this verse, the prototype of all subsequent *teshuva*, the return was immediate, instantaneous, overwhelming. It had no detectable motivation. One does not know by what—or by whom—it was provoked. And, at the same time, it was not a calling but rather the destruction of a blockage: Something had separated Moses from his brethren, and the wall collapsed. And the breach was there, gaping, and the leap was irreversible.

What was special about Moses' awakening, what made his "going out unto his brethren" a prototype of the Exodus, was that God was completely absent throughout the long first period of the process. The calling of Moses would come later, at the Burning Bush, but, before the incandescence of the vertical dialogue, for nearly forty years Moses' dealings with his brethren were exclusively on the horizontal plane. They were secular. No metaphysical absolutes: The relationship was a social one. What actuated Moses in the awakening of his Jewish identity was the absolute of justice. It was his goad and his obsession. All we see of him at this stage in the Bible is a series of scenes in which Moses, faced with injustice, explodes, gets angry, intervenes, causes a row, protests, acts. He throws himself on the Egyptian overseer who strikes the Jew, and kills him. He involves himself in a quarrel between Jews and attempts to straighten it out. He brandishes *J'accuse* and *La Verité en marche*. The Midrash goes further and shows him associating himself with the sufferings of his brethren, sharing their labors and their burdens. Here, in essence, are the ancient and modern forms of Jewish solidarity.

But when Moses was forced to realize that his efforts were vain, that his brethren did not want his arm of justice, that they suspected him of being a kapo sold to their murderers when in fact the murderers had condemned him to death, he began another phase of his return to Jewish identity. He quitted his brethren and went out towards humanity, saving strangers—the daughters of Jethro the Midianite—from the violent hands of the Midianite shepherds. Here we see the dual nature of the Jewish instinct for justice. Moses the Jew is a perpetually restless individual whom injustice draws like a magnet. At one moment, here he is at the service of Jewish justice and of that exclusively, and at another moment, here he is at the service of universal human justice and of that exclusively. Now he was willing to face death to save his brethren, and now he risked his life to save humanity.

HE WHO HAD CALLED OTHERS
GETS HIS CALL

He had been the watchdog of all the flocks in the world. He had sounded the alarm bell and given warning. Now, more out of disillusionment than out of necessity, he thought that the time had come for retirement. He took his father-in-law's flocks to the backside of the desert, hoping to be alone.

"Moses, Moses!" He who so often had given the call was suddenly called. The bush burned and was not consumed. Yes, it's the image of my conscience which burns and is not consumed, despite the ashes in which I have covered it. But what can this Voice be which takes hold of my conscience, badgers it and seeks to transform its flame into a conflagration?

A touching Midrash lifts the veil on this matter. What, then, was the ruse whereby God traced a path to the consciousness of this Jew who had chosen to be alone, separated from his brethren and separated from God—from a God of Whom he could have sworn an oath that he had never heard His voice? It was not by means of the sounding Voice of the Almighty, for it overwhelms and reduces to nothing. It was not by means of the tenuous Voice of the Omnipresent, for it is fleeting and elusive like the wind. The Voice used by God to call Moses, to bring him back to his Jewish identity, was the voice of his father. "Is it Amram, Amram, my father? Is it you? Are you still alive?"

"No, your father Amram is dead, but the God of your father Amram is always living."

Jewish consciousness awakens through the re-emergence of a Jewish childhood hidden in the deepest levels of the un- and sub-conscious. What Moses heard was the voice of the roots he had extirpated, of the family he had half forgotten, of the Jewish origins for which he had substituted an Egyptian, Midianite, purely human identity. But in the Jew there is something still more simple than humanity, something naive, pure, innocent: childhood. The tales of my mother Yohebed, the stories of my father Amram, the songs of my sister Miriam, the lessons of my brother Aaron. The

Sabbath: the reception of the Sabbath, its melody, its rest. Its benediction of twenty-four hours as against six days of a dog's life, of grousing, of insults, of blows, of despondency, of deportation and of death. A Jewish childhood: the cradle of a promised life just as Jewish history is the cradle of a Promised Land.

> It dandles you in so maternal a manner and awakens you so suddenly that even Jews who have long abandoned the faith of their fathers . . . feel moved from the bottom of their hearts when these ancient accents which are so familiar . . . by chance strike their ears. . . .

Heinrich Heine

THE TYPOLOGY OF THE DESERT

The desert: in universal thinking a symbol of emptiness, but where the Jewish destiny is concerned, the symbol of an overflowing fullness.

The nomads of the desert cross the sands without leaving a trace either in history or in the memory. It is precisely because they have no history that the nomads are happy: they forget where they have come from, they do not know where they are going. The oases retain them long enough for them to refill their goatskins, and then they continue on their way, a slow caravan of camels, crossing over from an emerging horizon to a disappearing horizon—that is, unless, somewhere along their path, the sands cover them and they disappear forever, for all eternity ignorant of time and its tensions.

Such also are the hermits of the desert, cloistered in the self-sufficiency of their asceticism. Cut off from the world, they feed themselves on carobs and litanies and make a perpetual journey around themselves until death embraces them and they disappear forever, for all eternity ignorant of time and its tensions.

Such, finally, are the *poètes maudits*, the "damned" (or blessed) poets, attaching their dreams to the hells (paradises) of a journey in the desert, where all is beauty, *luxe, calme, et volupté* (luxury, calm, and voluptuousness) until opium delivers them forever, for all eternity ignorant of time and its expectations.

At the opposite extreme, there is the desert of the biblical man, the desert of the Jew. The Jew, too, is a nomad. He is more than a nomad, he is gone astray. He, too, is a hermit. He is more than a hermit, he is isolated. He, too, is a poet. He is more than a poet, he is a prophet. But the desert of this straying nomad is woven into the fabric of time; the desert of this isolated hermit is inserted into the framework of a place; the desert of this poet-prophet is provided with the substance of a vision. Time-place-vision are for the Jew a permanent encounter with a tension, a temptation, an expectation. The tension rives him, the temptation tears him asunder, the expectation binds him up, and the coincidence of this triple thread makes up the knotted drama of his desert.

The Jewish symbolism of the desert has its roots in a piece of history whose context is simple and well known: the forty years covered in the Bible by the narrative which extends from the end of the Book of Genesis to the beginning of the Book of Joshua. For the Jew, however, these roots, although they have given birth to symbols, are not in themselves symbolic: They are existential. In each of their variations, the signs, the themes, the myths of the desert concern the Jew in his actual personal adventure. When a Jew questions himself about his identity, he feels himself questioned by the desert, assailed by a series of questions left by the biblical desert in the collective memory of the Jewish people. It can also happen that the Jew ceases to question himself about his identity. He believes himself to have attained the security of a certainty, which can be that of a plenitude or that of emptiness. The certainty of being what he is, quite simply a Jew, for Jewishness is his true identity, or the certainty of being what he is, quite simply a man, having divested himself of whatever Jewishness had added to his identity. But then the desert surges up from the depths of the memory. With its tensed cords it lays hold of one's mental equilibrium and shakes the Jew to his most hidden recesses. The initial key of the full score of the Jewish drama is set in the desert. "Every man has the duty of considering himself as if he himself had come out of Egypt," says the ancient narrative of the Exodus, repeated each Passover eve by Jewish tradition. "Each Jew," one should add, "each Jew one day has the dizzying certainty that it is just as if he himself had experienced the adventure of the desert." Just as it is not only ceremonially that the Jew re-situates himself in the night of the Exodus but it presents itself in the form of an existential problem, so he is not only intellectually involved in the symbolism of the desert, but it confronts him in the aggressiveness of the problem of his identity.

Where are you, Jew, in any one (or in all) of the multiple and complex type-situation of the biblical desert of your being?

Is it the situation of the horizontal tension? Are you stretched on the taut rope extending from Exodus to Entry, living in the ambiguity of a glance backwards to Egypt together with a glance forward to Canaan? Does this simultaneous prospect reconcile the contrary poles of Abandonment and Promise or does it make you suffer from being as far removed from Reality as from the Ideal?

Is it the situation of the vertical tension? Are you stretched on the taut rope between Sinai and the steppes, between the lofty, austere voice of the Ten Commandments and the frenzied orgiastic debauchery of the Golden

Calf? Are you listening to the voice of your Unique God or engaged in the fabrication of one of your numerous idols?

Is it the situation of the diagonal tension between the economy of the fleshpots and that of *manna?* In that of the psychic tension between a return to slavery and the confrontation of liberty? In that of the political tension between patience and going all out, between submission and rebellion, between compromise and the absolute?

Have you dreamed and explored in the desert? Have you gone from one end to the other like Joshua and Caleb, or like Miriam and Aaron, did you give way before the end? Have you, like Moses, known the burning heat of the Bush, the intoxication of the Word, anger at frustrations in the desert? Have you carried the Tablets of the Covenant? Have you shattered them? Have you gathered up the broken fragments of the Covenant and hewn new ones with your own hands? Have you written nothing on the new Tablets except what was written on the old ones? Have you broken the chain of tradition or have you taken it up again?

At the ultimate limits of the desert, when your gaze embraced with love and longing the land of the Promise, did Nebo rise up as an impassable barrier and was it there that a grave opened up for you eternally whose place no one but you will ever know?

In the desert, did you die, and, in the desert, were you born?

ISRAEL, A COMPANY OF UNLIMITED LIABILITY

"That we may also be like all the nations" (Deuteronomy 17:14, I Samuel 8:20). The desire to be "like the others" is expressed in the Bible in connection with the concept of kingship. It was on the political level that Israel dreamed of creating its City, its *polis*, on the same model as all the others. Israel—a society without problems, without questions, or answers! The Land of Israel, a country like the others, without a history, without troubles!

It is worse than a dream: It's amnesia (loss of memory). It is worse than forgetfulness: It is madness.

And as for the mad thought which cometh into your mind, in that ye say: we will be as the nations, as the families of the countries, to serve wood and stone. As I live, saith the Lord God, surely with a mighty hand, and with an outstretched arm, and with fury poured out, will I rule over you (Ezekiel 20:32–33).

It is as it was in former times: I alone, the living God, with a mighty hand and with an outstretched arm, obliged your ancestor Jacob to ally himself with Me for all eternity (Genesis 32).

Having only just escaped Laban and seeing Esau coming towards him with his four hundred horsemen, Jacob had a moment of hesitation. He sent his wives, his children, and his household over the river Jabbok, intending to follow them and, together with them, to make a detour, avoiding the encounter with Esau.

That night, Jacob refused to make the effort: He rejected the pull towards absolute Time. He sought refuge in his own time, wished to retain the freedom of his own destiny, wanted a life like that of other people, recoiled before a divine vocation and thought only of himself. He wanted to remain Jacob.

But that same night, before he had taken the final step of crossing the Jabbok and turning a deaf ear to his calling, when he was alone, then, despite himself, the Unknown One rose up and obliged him to engage in a struggle. It was a tragic struggle of Jewish existence which wanted to refuse to enter into the absolute but was forced to do so, and it could never again be satisfied until it had won the triumph of the absolute through blessing. Jacob came out of this struggle wounded, defeated in his desire to live a life for himself but a victor in his divine vocation: limping towards his encounter with Esau, but as *Israel,* a link in the chain of the Absolute, the bearer of God—El—in his name.

Jacob had not been able to remain his own master. The absolute took hold of him in order to thrust him forward into a self-transcendence. Israel become a people was not able to remain its own master. The universal took hold of it in order to propel it into a self-transcendence.

Here one has deliberate solitude, solitude experienced, solitude and uniqueness as major signs of Jewish identity, but also the desire "to be like the others" as a major sign of the loss of Jewish identity.

Diagonally—*be'emtsa,* as the Maharal of Prague would say—a fellowship with the nations as equals, yet preserving one's vocation, actual or utopian, of an absolute of the universal. Israel is thrust onto the level of being able to reply to the questions which trouble humanity, is provided with an unlimited power to give utterance to the Voice of God which it carries in itself, in its very name, to respond—to show responsibility. Israel, a company with unlimited liability:

In those days it shall come to pass that ten men shall take hold, out of all the languages of the nations, even shall take hold of the skirt of him that is a Jew, saying, We will go with you, for we have heard that God is with you (Zechariah 8:23).

6

The Prophetical Metadrama

THE FORCED RETURN

If the idea of return is the least tragic concept in Greek thought, in biblical thought, on the contrary, it corresponds to the exact moment when the drama turns into a tragedy. Human time, in the true sense of the word, with its unique character and history, does not concern men, the form of whose lives is circular. The cyclical theme of the eternal return is the death of history. Conceivably, it eliminates pain: "Happy the man who, like Ulysses, has made a fair voyage and then returned . . . " But at the same time it divests time of its rhythm and history of its content.

Jonah also made a fair voyage. Sirens, fiercer than those met by Ulysses, it is true, tempted and delayed him in his journey towards Tarshish: a hurricane, a stormy plunge in the sea, an execution by drowning, three days in the Fish's belly. Wow! All's well that ends well. The embarkation for Tarshish was only a diversion. Jonah went back to Nineveh where he ought to have gone in the first place. So he too returned.

Only, it was a forced return. When he finally reached Nineveh, Jonah was unhappy, even more unhappy than he had been among the lethal waves. He was unhappy to the point of wanting to die. It was because his voyage had turned out to be a tragedy. Before the return, there had been a rupture. Ulysses returned to the point to which he wanted to return and to which he should have returned. Thus, the circle was completed. This circle protected him against any new adventure, while Jonah, on the other hand, went back to the place which he wished to avoid and ought to have avoided. He wished to avoid it. His embarkation for Tarshish was a flight, an Exodus in the night, towards the antipodes, towards nothingness, in order to get away from God! He ought to have avoided it: His return to Nineveh proved to be useless. Come to proclaim the overthrow of Nineveh, Jonah learned what he most feared: Nineveh was saved! A journey for nothing, a missed return. The circle remains open. For Jonah, the return was a Genesis, something new—we shall never know what. The page has remained blank in the Bible. Perhaps Jonah himself was never able to read his fate in these non-lines in the Bible.

This was the tragedy of the prophetic return. There can be no joining without a preceding rupture. There can be no joining without the risk of another rupture. It would be a continual tossing to and fro if the prophets had not placed this tragedy within the continuity of a discontinuous time-scheme: that of conjugal knowledge which the prophets made the symbol of their personal history, of the history of Israel, and of the history, finally, of mankind and the world. I shall return to this later.

THE KINGDOM OF A GOD WHOSE THRONE IS DOWN HERE

Between the longing for non-being for which the cosmos is nothing and the aspiration towards being other, for which the human world is everything, the Covenant claims that the world with all its cosmic and human elements does indeed exist, but only through its relationship with God. Non-being and being other are reduced to the status of symbols, images, desires: They cannot have any reality in themselves, for God is co-present in everything. When they appear, they are modalities of this co-presence, tensions which express in an acute manner the presence of God, Being by means of God.

This is the significance of the omnipotence of God, of the panentheism that is the cornerstone of the metaphysics of biblical man. The metaphysics of an encounter in which paradoxes spring forth with a prodigality which is as blinding as it is dazzling: fear and protection, the abyss and the bridge, the break and the connection, separation and reunion, exile and return. In order to describe the salient points of this encounter, one must first describe their forms, for these points are sometimes atoms and sometimes galaxies, and, nearly always, both of these at one and the same time.

THE MORPHOLOGY OF RHYTHM

"Frightened as a Jew" they used to say in the Middle Ages. Which Jew of the twentieth century has not experienced fear? The fear produced by history which has seized him by the throat, and the fear produced by the reading of history in the pages of the Bible (Leviticus 26, Deuteronomy 28) written three thousand years ago and even a bit more, as though the Bible had spread in advance, across the centuries and millennia, the net in which the Jewish destiny was to be held, or as if it was not Moses (or editor R, O learned doctors of the Higher Criticism!) who had written them but I, André Neher, a Jew of the twentieth century, and a few million of my brethren in religion (or race or community or nation or society or Jewishness, O learned analysts of Jewish identity!) as pages of my diary between 1940 and 1944. The rhythm of concordance between the description and the reality, between the reading and the experience, between the Bible and my destiny appears to have, in itself, something hallucinatory about it.

But there is also something else, something extra. The rhythm of a discordance within these same pages of the Bible—the colossal advance of a bloodthirsty army and the timid silence of the night, the infernal sound of slaughter when men are murdered and the rustle of the leaf carried by the breeze, the agony of hunger on the roads of exile and the satiety of the Land which rests at last, fear of night falling and fear of day rising. The elements of a rhythm with three components, where the first two shun and pursue one another, graze against one another and interweave, cut one another and join, and come to a resolution in the third factor, now syncopated, now silent, now overwhelming, but always present: that of God.

The Divine Contract: this expression was my father's. Man possessed the terms of a contract drawn up in a rational manner with a table of contents and an index, but God erased the contents and shattered inertia with the omnipresence of His Index (finger). The senile and puerile concept of the finger of God in all things, a naive and simplistic belief in Providence, here they are suddenly matured, grown grave, tragic, irrefutable, simultaneously inscribed in the Bible deciphered by the Jew and in the absurdity which tattoos a number on the Jew's arm at Auschwitz.

PHANTASMS OF THE CURVATURE

One day, David wanted to run away from God. He had suffered God's blows in his mind, his body, his movements, and his words. He suffered from being merely the Golem of God:

Psalm 139

O Lord, thou knowest my downsitting and my uprising, thou understandest my thought afar off.

Thou compassest my path and my lying down, and are acquainted with all my ways.

For there is not a word in my tongue, but, lo, O Lord, thou knowest it altogether.

Thou hast beset me behind and before, and laid thine hand upon me.

So, he took his route, but his route proved to be a rout! God remained the limitless limit of his journey:

Whither shall I go from thy spirit? Or whither shall I flee from thy presence?

If I ascend up into heaven, thou art there: if I make my bed in the netherworld, behold, thou art there.

If I take the wings of the morning, and dwell in the uttermost parts of the sea;

Even there shall thy hand lead me, and thy right hand shall hold me.

If I say, surely the darkness shall cover me; even the night shall be light about me.

Yea, the darkness hideth not from thee, but the night shineth as the day: the darkness and the light are both alike to thee.

A puppet, a marionette, held by invisible threads from the finger of God: Such is the Jew. A sleepwalker, or rather, in the very words of the Divine Contract, "a blind man groping in darkness." In the double impenetrability of the night, the infinite circles of an obscurity in which the Jew hits his head against God. After David, Amos said the same thing: there is no place of refuge, no hiding place, no escape. Everywhere one comes up against God:

Not one of them shall flee away, not one of them shall be delivered. Though they dig into hell, thence shall mine hand take them; though they climb up to heaven, thence will I bring them down. And though they hide themselves in the top of Carmel, I will search and take them out thence (Amos 9:1–3).

It is still acceptable if it is God Himself who barricades the path of escape with His own presence, but the fear becomes obsessive and the dream a nightmare when God takes on the form of slave drivers, kapos, dogs that watch, search, seize by the scruff of the neck, arrest, deport, and deliver up to selection and death:

Though they be hid from my sight at the bottom of the sea, thence will I command the serpent, and he shall bite them; and though they go into captivity before their enemies, thence will I command the sword, and it shall slay them. (Amos 9:3–4).

Command the sword? It is still acceptable if it is God Himself who wields the sword. To be slain by God—that still has a certain panache, but God entrusts His divine swords to one or another of His many servants.

The unacceptable idea that Pharaoh, Haman, Torquemada, Hitler—the practitioners of genocide throughout history—were servants of God would never have entered the sphere of Jewish theological nightmares if Jeremiah the prophet had not enunciated it, on God's dictation, in connection with a practitioner of genocide worthy of figuring in the very incomplete list which I have just drawn up, namely "Nebuchadnezzar my servant!" (Jeremiah 25:9 and 27:6).

Nebuchadnezzar, that "great hammer of the earth," pounding peoples and empires, chariots and horsemen, massacring men and women, children and old people, youths and maidens, shepherds and flocks, ploughmen and teams of oxen, princes and ministers, and devastating trees and pastures— he was only a docile instrument in the hands of the great Ironsmith who wielded him!

If that, indeed, is the case, then anything is possible. The psychic intoxication attains the proportions of a myth which has left a very deep trace in history—the myth of accursedness. It has been thought that a people thus seized upon by God and his predictions can ultimately only be a people subjected to God through the chains of His malediction:

> All these curses shall come upon thee, and overtake thee:
> Cursed shalt thou be in the city, and cursed shalt thou be in the field.
> Cursed shall be thy basket and thy store.
> Cursed shall be the fruit of thy body, and the fruit of thy land, the increase of thy kine, and the flocks of thy sheep.
> Cursed shalt thou be when thou comest in, and cursed shalt thou be when thou goest out. (Deuteronomy 28:15–19).

THE JEWISH MYSTERY

Of all human communities, the Christian is the one which has taken upon itself to elaborate in the most systematic manner the myth of the accursed Jewish people. Christianity thus followed in the footsteps of Balak, king of Moab, who asked Bileam, the seer of Midian, to "curse this people" in order that it could be annihilated. Christianity thus prepared the way for the Shoa, the final solution of this nightmare through the complete and total extermination of the accursed people in the twentieth century by the Third Reich under our very eyes.

The mystery of Israel! In the vocabulary of Christian theology, this is a concept which is given a place next to a number of dogmas which are also mysterious: the mystery of the Incarnation, the dogma of the Trinity, the mystery of the Immaculate Conception. Thus, the Christian can take part, sometimes even with serenity, in Jew-hunting—a form of hunting in which persecution by men can be synonymous with pursuit by God. If the Christian is not always among the hunters, he is, at any rate, rarely among the prey. But the Jew, always hunted, cornered, and wounded in body and soul, how is he to act in the face of this mystery? The Jew, whose entry onto the scene of history, but also whose exit, are marked with a similar malediction?

Two possibilities are suggested by the Divine Contract itself.

The first, tragically manifested by Elie Wiesel in his work of testimony—*madness:* " . . . and thou shalt be mad for the sight of thine eyes which thou shalt see" (Deuteronomy 28:34).

And the second, used by Elie Wiesel in his work of testimony as a counterweight to madness—and yet, for all that, *remembrance:* " . . . And yet for all that, when they be in the land of their enemies, I will not cast them away, neither will I abhor them, to destroy them utterly, and to break my covenant with them: For I am the Lord their God, but I will remember . . . " (Leviticus 26:44).

Could it be that this whirlwind of words casting the Jew back into the madness of silence and nothingness was nevertheless an act of remembrance on the part of God?

Each one asked himself in the silence of his nothingness
And was it, in reality, the diligence of the Living God?

Benjamin Fondane

THE CONJUGAL MEMORY

Memory, remembrance: experiences predicted for the Jew some three thousand and more years ago, things experienced by the Jew some thirty and a few more years ago. A tri-millennial prediction read in the tri-millennial Bible of Moses by the Jew who lived thirty years ago. For the Jew it was a concordance of life and literature, and for God a remembrance embracing the Scriptures, life and literature within the unbreakable continuity of a time scheme in which yesterday, today, and tomorrow come together with a fulgurating simultaneity. At the very moment when Moses was chiseling the Covenant in the columns of the Bible, he was sculpting its perpetuity in the memory of God.

What does God remember? The Covenant: the Covenant, with its thousand flames and myriad sparks. They rise from the rock of history hewn with the hammer-strokes of the divine Word. The Covenant of the Patriarchs, Abraham, Isaac, and Jacob, the Covenant of the Rainbow, the Covenant of the departure from Egypt. The Covenant of the return from the Diaspora; the Covenant of Adam, the Covenant of the Messiah, and, underlying all of them, binding these changing Covenants one to another, the Covenant with Israel: "Yea, a woman may forget the child of her womb, yet will I not forget thee" (Isaiah 49:15).

Can a woman forget her suckling babe, cease to love (*merahem*) the child of her womb, cease to carry the child in the womb (*rehem*) of her own being when the existence of the child is already detached from that of its mother? Well, a woman may be able to do such a thing, but I, God, am not!

In no other passage is the seriousness of the Covenant brought home so strikingly. Is not human wisdom aware that everything that perishes is only a symbol (Goethe) and that human love itself, like the whole of human existence, is only symbolic? Precisely: If the human reality confirms its purely symbolic nature and demonstrates by means of experience how fragile and transitory human love is ("Were a woman to forget"), there remains the meta-reality of meta-human love, of the love of God for Israel, which is not a transient symbol but a symbol of eternity: "*I* will not forget."

Over and beyond the Pharaohs, the Nebuchadnezzars, the Hamans, the Hitlers, and within the exiles, the stakes, the gas chambers—satanic invitations to delirium and insanity—there remains the immortal reality of the Love of God for Israel, there remains the Covenant enshrined in the meta-symbol of conjugal love.

The reader will understand if I refrain here from a further analysis of the conjugal symbolism in the Bible. From my very first books to the twentieth—which is this one—I have expended heaven knows how much ink and energy and emotion in attempting to show how original, how amazing, how revolutionary the conjugal symbolism of the Bible was and to how great a degree this contribution of the prophets to human thought has enabled the Jewish people to survive, and, by means of this survival, has enabled the human race to exist. I refer the reader to the index of my books. He or she will find under the heading "Conjugal (symbolism): cf. Love" or something of that nature, an enumeration of the pages which, I hope, will be one of the lasting fruits of my Jewish reading of the Bible and of my Jewish existence through and within it.

Now in a few brief verses, now in vast frescoes covering several chapters and always in accordance with a consistent terminology whose outlines and characteristics are to be found everywhere throughout the Bible, the prophets compare history to a touching drama of conjugal love and its vicissitudes. God the husband (*ish*) and Israel the wife (*isha*) search for one another, unite, lose one another, and find one another once more through childhood, puberty, betrothal, marriage, separation, divorce, widowhood, and new encounters. The essential quality of the drama and its vicissitudes is incompletion, but the power of resurgence is inexhaustible. It is the tangible image of the dynamics of the living and eternal God.

In an attempt to express this resurgence, prophetic language used those means which the varieties of conjugal symbolism placed at its disposal: giving birth in pain, midnight anguish, awaiting the dawn, the solitary cry and dialogue. History is conceived as abortion, sterility, losing oneself in the darkness, obliteration in the depths, asphyxiation and silence; sometimes it is seduction, jealousy, violence, rape, prostitution, debauchery. It is always, at a peak moment which is a sort of ultimate of resurgence, the passing of the midnight hour, a rising out of the lowest depths, a song on the reefs of the shipwreck, reunion, comfort, repentance (synonymous in the Bible with consolation), remembrance, non-forgetfulness.

The forms in which the drama is unfolded are as various as the situations of the protagonists. Now one has a story, a narrative which allows the husband, God, to stir things up, and the wife, Israel, to respond. Now one has an experiential, psychodramatic form. One prophet, Isaiah, gave his children names which symbolized the various directions of history: catastrophe, return, redemption. Another, Jeremiah, had to accept celibacy as the sign of the sterilization of a course of history whose future fecundation he could only imagine. Still another, Ezekiel, suddenly became a widower, and it was through this experience of death that he was able to envisage the resurrection of the dry bones. Finally, Hosea had to re-live, through marriage with a prostitute, all the deviations of Israelite Canaanism. History thus remained suspended above a void: His children carried negation in their very names—*lo ruhama,* not loved; *lo ammi,* not my people. God is defined in terms of negation, and Israel also. The Covenant is held together from below on the level of a cessation of history and in the dimension of a rupture: "For you are not my people and I will not be your God." But this void, however, is crossed. Through a mysterious shift of the Covenant from negative to positive, the denial of this negation becomes once again an affirmation of love: "Say ye unto your brethren, My people, and to your sisters, Beloved!"

Obviously, it is not exclusively a conjugal relationship. It can also be a parental one. In the story of Hosea, Israel simultaneously plays the role of the wife and that of the three children. The leap from rupture to reunification creates at one and the same time a new betrothal and a new birth.

Isaiah was also aware of this secret: "As one whom his mother comforteth, so will I comfort you, and ye shall be comforted in Jerusalem" (Isaiah 66:13).

And under the eternally nuptial canopy of maternal love—*rahamim* (from *rehem,* the womb), a term employed by Isaiah in the verse we quoted earlier (49:15)—God and Israel are united in an indestructible co-presence. The term *rahamim* defines love here in its essential gravity and truth. One being can, if need be, separate himself definitively from another being, lose sight of him, forget him. The heart may forget, but a mother cannot forget.

But, even if a mother could forget, I, God, shall not forget thee, Israel. The conjugal-cum-parental metaphor guarantees the meta-historical character of the Covenant.

There is thus no place in biblical thought for theological ideas such as degeneration, rejection, malediction, for is not a fall an infant's first step towards the welcoming arms of life? Does not a fruit in detaching itself from the tree begin the cycle of its existence? Are not a mother's cries in the throes of childbirth the first stammerings of a maternal blessing? Since nothing is forgotten, everything always exists in memory, in more than memory, in the super-memory of God, where the eternal history of the Jew is concerned.

The key term *nehama* throws a light on this fundamental polarity of memory and super-memory, for this term designates both repentance and consolation: *teshuva* in life—surrection, rising up—and the *teshuva* after physical or spiritual death—resurrection. In order to understand this concept, one has to recognize the fact that God repents. The idea of God repenting seems so abhorrent that it is often challenged in the Bible itself (Numbers 23:19, I Samuel 15:29). And yet, God does repent: of having created humanity (Genesis 6:6), of having chosen Saul (I Samuel 15:11), of having rejected and condemned the children of Israel (Exodus 32:14). This repentance expresses the whole anthropomorphic reaction of regret, disappointment, weariness, "That's enough!" and at the same time, the opposite attitude—consolation, consolidation, pulling oneself together, energy, willpower, getting back to the task, hope, "And yet, for all that!" These two attitudes of "Enough!" and "For all that" are both contained in this biblical *teshuva* of God.

This simultaneity is also to be seen in the biblical *teshuva* of man, through the perpetually re-soldering effect of a Covenant that no forgetfulness can ever break. Nothing is potentially more whole than a break, for it is in the break that the virtue of wholeness resides. When a man in the Bible says "I am abandoned," at the same time and by means of the same word (*azav* in Hebrew) he says, "I am gathered in." Abandonment and ingathering belong together, not because of the compensatory healing effect of the passage of time but through the dialectic of their inseparable relationship, of their interconnection with the Covenant. When a man in the Bible takes a step in the direction of return, it is a going towards a God who has already returned towards him. When a man in the Bible takes a step in the direction of flight, it is a flight towards a God for whom fleeing is a convex form of return. When a man in the Bible wants to go far away, he goes towards a God who is nearer far away than he is close at hand (Jeremiah 23:23). When a man in the Bible is pulverized, it is through the hammer stroke of the divine Word. The rock of Jewish existence is then splintered into a thousand sparks (Jeremiah 23:29). Light is sown for the

Righteous. In full daylight it is the sunshine of the world. Thousands of sparks are sown through the pulverization of he who returns, the *ba'al teshuva*. In the world's skies they shine in the deep night like galaxies of stars.

Part Three

FROM DENIAL TO REAFFIRMATION

"And every star that fails finds with its deepest fall the way back to the eternal home."

Nelly Sachs

7

The Variants of Dis-assimilation

THE ABSOLUTE IMPASSE

As an apotheosis of his meta-theater, the inventor of sociodrama and meta-Freudian psychoanalysis, Jacob Levi Moreno, used the scenario of the traditional Seder. In the Seder, all is ritual improvisation, for from the beginning the invitation is given out: "Whoever is hungry, let him come and eat, and whoever feels the need, let him come and celebrate the Passover!" and anyone may suddenly enter, the Friend, the Stranger, the Messiah, but also Amalek, absolute evil. And, a little later, as though to bring out the quality of the unexpected, "the door is opened"—the door through which the Awaited One may enter, but also the Unawaited One, the "anti," disrupting the magic of the evening with the calumny of ritual murder, as Heinrich Heine imagined in his *Rabbi of Bacharach*. It is a door, also, through which someone, instead of entering, can suddenly leave and slip away into the night, as Israel Zangwill imagined in his *Had Gadya*.

The French version of Zangwill's *Had Gadya* was published for the first time by Charles Péguy in his *Cahiers de la Quinzaine* in 1904. Neither the date nor the place of publication were fortuitous. At that time, one was still in the midst of the Dreyfus Affair in which Charles Péguy had played so important a role next to his friend Bernard Lazare, who had just died, and in which also, Israel Zangwill had played so important a role next to his friend Theodor Herzl, who had just died.

Bernard Lazare and Theodor Herzl were two Jews who returned to the Jewish hearth through the half-open door of the Seder. They were two victims of the "anti" whom the magnetic attraction of the Seder helped to convince that the assimilation of the Jew is impossible.

The anonymous hero of Zangwill's *Had Gadya* was the Jew for whom dis-assimilation was impossible. This lost child also wanted to go home. Disappointed, disillusioned, battered, and exhausted by the outside world in which he had vainly sought to obtain everything that a man can, the door to the Jewish world opened to him at the moment when, in the House of his

Father, his father began the curious recitation with which the Seder ends: Had Gadya, Had Gadya! And it was through this song which, from a single little kid bought by my father for two *zuzim* leads to the Justice of the Holy One, Blessed be He—a sure, necessary, absolute justice, and yet flouted, trampled on, betrayed (O Dreyfus, O Zola, O Pharaoh, O Auschwitz!)—it was through this song that the consciousness of the returning son divested itself. It divested itself of all that it had gathered in the world outside and yet was sure that it could no longer find anything within. This dialectic of without and within stifled this lost Jew until he reached an absolute impasse. Within, it was too late to return, unless it was to gather in the "meta" of an ancient song, as old as the Jews themselves, the painful impression that in the Father's House there is room enough for everyone except oneself. Without, there was no longer anything to be found except death—a plunge into the waters of a Venetian canal where the scene unwound:

> But as he sank for the last time, the mystery of the night and the stars and death mingled with a strange whirl of childish memories instinct with the wonder of life, and the immemorial Hebrew words of the dying Jew beat outwards to his gurgling throat: 'Hear, O Israel' . . .
>
> Through the open doorway floated down the last words of the hymn and the service . . . Had Gadya! Had Gadya! . . .

Nine years later, Charles Péguy published in these same *Cahiers de la Quinzaine* the first poems of Edmond Fleg's cycle *Écoute, Israel*. Here we have a thesis and antithesis centering on the six "immemorial words" of the Shema Israel: the thesis of the Jew to whom the "anti" of the Dreyfus Affair had restored the "meta" of his Jewish specificity, withdrawing him from assimilation, and the antithesis of the Jew whom the failure of assimilation leads to suicide.

TOO LATE: HEINRICH HEINE

People have wondered what Zangwill's prototype was for his *Had Gadya*. There were so many visionaries of the *Shoa* at the beginning of the twentieth century that Zangwill, who died in 1926, may possibly, like Franz Kafka and Jakob Wassermann, have been one of them. The fate of his anonymous hero of Venice was possibly a foretaste of that of Stefan Zweig, of Kurt Tucholski, of Walter Benjamin, and of so many others whom the Third Reich drove to suicide. Did not Stefan Zweig see a hint of return?

Did he not catch a glimpse of the fact that the absoluteness of the Hitlerian meaninglessness might conceivably—and ultimately—be given a significance by the Bible and Job? And yet, for all that, he chose suicide. Had Gadya, Had Gadya . . .

It is more generally believed, however, that Zangwill's model was Heine.

The "retraction" with which I began this book was, in fact, one among many others which were less serene, more tortured, tormented in a way that recalls the prophets of the Bible. Cantankerous, angry, and even blasphemous, Heine's outbursts showed that he had found, not a text but the corroboration of a text in the situation he was living through: that of Job on his dunghill. At the heart of the misery he was experiencing, Heine found himself in a profoundly biblical state of mind. A wretched, unhappy little man, he felt himself to be in the presence of the great and silent Interlocutor; racked by doubt and suffering, he sensed that this was the biblical form of faith. Through a misery drunk to the depths, as bitter as can be, yet slaking an infinite spiritual thirst, Judaism was restored to him.

However, he did not take it upon himself once more in a clearly-defined ritual act like that performed by Arnold Schönberg in 1933 in that same city of Paris where in 1853 Heine specifically asked that neither a Christian mass nor a Jewish *kaddish* should be said at his funeral. Clearly, his inner struggle had not ended when death overtook him three years later.

But the volcanic overflow of Heine's impossible assimilation, the way out drama of this Jew torn apart, could find its way out only in the incompleted. There are cases in which the last word of return was not said because it was simply not sayable. That was the case with Heine. Had Gadya, Had Gadya . . .

A ROAD WITHOUT A LANDSCAPE: BERNARD LAZARE

For Bernard Lazare, the journey was different. In writing *Le Fumier de Job* (Job's Dunghill), a work which was also unfinished and which demonstrated an atheist's return to the Bible, the author was not inspired by sickness, although it was written in conditions of physical wretchedness which recall Heine's sickbed-cum-burial vault and Job's biblical dunghill. The title of the book, which remained in a fragmentary condition, refers, as we know, not to Bernard Lazare's individual suffering but to "the national shame of the Jewish people." As in the case of the Dreyfus Affair which was a particular instance of it, Bernard Lazare demanded absolute truthfulness in the treatment of the Jewish question in general. In a letter in which he broke with Herzl, Bernard Lazare wrote:

Like all governments, you want to prettify the truth, to be the government of a people which looks clean, and the ultimate of duty for you is to avoid exposing the national points of shame. But I'm for exposing them, for displaying poor Job on his dunghill scratching his ulcers with a piece of broken bottle. We are dying from concealing our points of shame, from hiding them in deep cellars instead of bringing them out into the fresh air so that the strong sunlight will purify or cauterize them. Our people are wallowing in the most abject mire. We must pull up our sleeves and go out and find them where they are whining, where they are groaning, where they are suffering . . .

Le Fumier de Job is the jigsaw puzzle of this search, left incomplete because Bernard Lazare was overtaken by death. Several voices speak in this manuscript: the sentimental voice, the voice of the rationalist philosopher, and the voice of humanity "which considers Judaism a good point of departure." It will never be possible to determine with which voice Bernard Lazare himself identified: The polyphony reflected the multiplicty of paths which opened before him. When he broke with Herzl, it was not a break with Zionism as such, but only with the bourgeois and bureaucratic form of Zionism which rightly or wrongly Herzl embodied in the opinion of Bernard Lazare. Lazare continued to demand a Zionism which would be socialistic and anarchistic. The "meta" embodied in Zionism for this prophet was only a prefiguration, an approximation of a vaster, more universal "meta" which, through Zion, would reach the whole world, and through the Jew, the whole of humanity.

Who are you? What do you want to be? You are Jewish they tell you, and this word strikes your ear as a foreign name might strike it. You are Jewish: do you know what it is to be Jewish? Do like me: Learn it! You want to serve the world? Be yourself, develop your personality, and you will serve it well.

Thus, Judaism is regained as a "point of departure," as a springboard for the human. I said that at the time when death overtook him, a number of Jewish paths opened before Bernard Lazare, but in fact, in his development, he had not yet reached the point where choices are made. It was not only in theory that Judaism was a point of departure. The actual process of *teshuva* placed Bernard Lazare at a point very close to a point of departure, but this was in the final moments of a life in which the forceful and heroic contour of the line of return was more significant than the landscape in which it only manifested itself experimentally.

DIS-ASSIMILATION BY TRANSFERENCE

In one of the scattered notes of *Le Fumier de Job* there is an encounter between Bernard Lazare and Heinrich Heine. It consists of two quotations taken by the prophet of the Dreyfus Affair from Heine's enormous Jewish opus:

"I have evoked, by means of a powerful magic, the sufferings of a thousand years," said Heine, speaking of the Rabbi of Bacharach.

"He, too, Yehuda ben Halevi, died at the feet of his beloved, and his dying head rested on the knees of Jerusalem."

These form part of Bernard Lazare's notes on his reading, which have not yet been worked up or placed in a general context, but are extremely enlightening. They associate two themes common to these two Jews whose paths of return I am attempting to trace: the sufferings of Israel and the love of Jerusalem, the "anti" of Amalek and the "meta" of Zionism. But if both these men shared these themes, what a difference there was in the use which either made of them in practice!

Bernard Lazare engaged himself in action. Because of Israel's sufferings, he allowed himself to be pulled hither and thither at the heart of the Affair; he rushed off to Romania. He was "involved." For the sake of Zionism, he went to Basle, to the Second Zionist Congress, received a hero's welcome and was co-opted into the Executive Committee where he remained for as long as its policies seemed to him to be in accordance with his principles. Heinrich Heine, on the other hand, was content with principles alone: His sole arm was the pen. He wrote poems and pamphlets but remained uninvolved in the political arena.

In this contrast we see an important aspect of return to Jewish identity. One of the possible forms of dis-assimilation is to wish to remain, is to remain purely theoretical in a way in which there is a strong feeling of "too late." There are gaps which cannot be filled because they are lost in an irrecoverable past. It is the Aleph swallowed up with the worlds which preceded the Beth of Bereshit. "In the beginning," in the Hebrew Bible, does not begin with the first letter of the alphabet but with the second.

So one gets a psychological transference. One says: If I had been born into the world of Aleph, I might have been Jewish—by birth, but being born, as I am, into the world of Beth, of duality, of division, I shall remain eternally dual and torn apart.

For the Jewish Zionist poet Heinrich Heine, Yehuda Halevi was the most outstanding object of this process of transference. About this prince of medieval Hebrew poetry, this songster of God and Zion, this Zionist who had the courage to leave the Eldorado of eleventh-century Spain in order to go and die at the foot of the walls of Jerusalem, Heine wrote a poem of dazzling beauty. Together with "Princess Sabbath," it forms the diptych of the "Hebrew Melodies" he wrote at the time of his *teshuva*.

But all we have of this *teshuva* is poetry, evasion, a voyage to which one abandons oneself only in a dream.

THE FRUSTRATION OF AN ELUSIVE FIGURE: FRANZ KAFKA

One can claim, like Max Brod, that Franz Kafka found a path of return—that of Zionism. But Zionism, for Kafka, was never a subject for serious reflection, for profound analysis, which allows us to claim, in contradiction to Max Brod, that Kafka was not really a Zionist.

One may also discern, like Max Brod, another path of return in Kafka—Yiddish culture, for which he had an undeniable infatuation. But Yiddish culture never took Kafka away from the roots of his German culture, and Max Brod himself recognized that Kafka never really became "Yiddishized."

But whatever was "really" in the case of Kafka? In Kafka nothing is significant except for Kafka: Nothing transcends the Kafkean immanence. No phrase of Kafka can define him better than the one chosen by Marthe Robert as the title of her exhaustive study of Kafka's Judaism: "Alone, like Franz Kafka."

Alone in his present moment, Kafka engaged in combat with himself, with the Jewish fraction of his being, overwhelmed with the traumatism of his father. What he took out of it could not be transposed, beyond today's struggle, to a tomorrow. In focusing the struggle on his past, he disorganized even further whatever within him was already chaotic. He added to the disorientation of his capacities, and, by so doing, limited all the more his aspirations.

Hence, Kafka's infatuation with two special areas of the Jewish promise: Yiddish culture and Zionism. These were erratic infatuations, for they gave Kafka only a strong sense of the impossibility of ever realizing them. The undeniable fact that Kafka's literary language was German turned his incapacity of becoming a Yiddishistic Jew into a gnawing frustration. The other undeniable, although painful, fact of a precarious state of health which rendered any long journey a mortal danger, made the prospect of his becoming a Zionist kibbutznik a tormentingly unrealizable ideal. He refused the invitations to travel offered with friendly insistence by Hugo and Elsa Bergmann, for he knew that he could never reach Palestine except on the map. The roots of Kafka's non-realizations lay in the ontological limitations of his own person.

8

The Challenge Accepted

BENJAMIN FONDANE

Throughout this book appears the name of Benjamin Fondane. There is a silhouette of him in the Prologue and there are a number of references and quotations from his works. My readers, moreover, can find his name and extracts from his texts and poems in most of my previous books. This is sufficient demonstration of Benjamin Fondane's position in my spiritual universe.

However, I owe my readers an admission. I first came across the name of this philosopher and poet whose thought has so strongly influenced me, and the whole of whose work was previous to the tragic date of October 2, 1944, when he perished in the gas chambers of Auschwitz, only following the Liberation, in 1945. But every line he wrote has since marked and accompanied me. A study of *Le Lundi Existentiel* in 1947 led me to a reading of the works published by Fondane before the war (*Rimbaud le Voyou, La Conscience Malheureuse, Ulysse, Titanic,* and *Faux Traité d'esthétique*) and those which were published after his death (*Baudelaire et l'Expérience du Gouffre,* 1947, "Rencontre avec Léon Chestov," preface to volume three of the works of Shestov, 1966, and *Super Flumina Babylonis,* 1965). In this last collection of poems there was a fragment entitled *La Mort de Dieu* (The Death of God) which had already been published in Edmond Fleg's *Anthologie Juive* (1951). But, above all, an astounding poem called *L'Exode* circulated from hand to hand from 1945 onwards. It was only much later that we learned that this text was only a fragment. The *Cahiers du Sud* published it in the collection *Le Génie d'Israël.* Together with others, I have done what I could to make this poem generally known (it is included in its partial form in my book *Moïse et la Vocation Juive,* with eight editions since 1956 and translations into six languages including Hebrew and Japanese). It was only in 1965 that, thanks to Claude Sernet, the poem was published in its entirety. Since then, studies on Fondane have multiplied: The journal *Non Lieu* devoted an issue to him in 1978 and Bernard Chouraqui gave him a chapter in *Le Scandale Juif*.

If I give all these details, it is because I am afraid that, despite the present dissemination of the name of Benjamin Fondane, there will no doubt be a large number of readers who will read his name here for the first time, just as I only met it for the first time after October 2, 1944 . . .

And also because the experience of *teshuva*, in the sense which I have given it, has not, thus far, been sufficiently emphasized by interpreters of Fondane, but that is just what has fascinated me ever since my first spiritual encounter with this figure.

Turning Around Judaism Like a Moth

"Benjamin Fondane, an authentic Jewish poet," it has been written here and there, and that is correct, providing this authenticity is apprehended in all its complexity. In Benjamin Fondane, there is a sub-structure of Jewish fidelity, but also an irruption of Jewish identity as a completely new discovery.

From the time of his birth in Jassy, Romania, in 1898, until that of his death in the gas chambers of Auschwitz-Birkenau in 1944, Benjamin Wexler, who became Barbu Fundoianu (and then Benjamin Fondane on his emigration to France in 1923), never for a moment stopped declaring himself a son of the Jewish people. His position as a Jew was acquired in the cradle.

Jassy, at the end of the nineteenth century, was one of the centers of European Judaism. Half of its population was Jewish, amounting to more than a hundred thousand souls. Shemuel Joseph Agnon celebrated the renown of the city in many of his stories. The adolescence and youth of Benjamin Wexler were rooted in Jewish Romania. His maternal uncles, the three Schwartzfeld brothers, were historiographers and Hebraists of worldwide reputation. It was when living on his paternal grandfather's rural estate that he adopted his nom-de-plume Fondane, and after the First World War became one of the group of outstanding young Jewish contributors to Romanian poetry.

Like many of his friends, however, he was attracted to France, to which he now devoted his pen and his poetical and philosophical inspiration, and he went to live in Paris. Having gained French citizenship in 1939, he volunteered for service in the armed forces and was wounded in the Phony War. Innocent and a dreamer, he thought himself a man like any other, pleased to share with the others the joys, but also the misfortunes of the human condition, although without renouncing Judaism as the price of this sharing. But his Judaism belonged to the sphere of thought and literature: It was not an *experienced* Judaism.

In the 1930s, when France was only beginning to discover Kierke-
gaard, Kafka, and more generally, the existential branch of philosophy,
Fondane was one of the writers who gave the most forceful expression to
the debt of the contemporary existentialist school to the Jewish Bible:
"Alone among books," he wrote,

> "the Bible cracks under the weight of an infinite possibility
> opened up to Man, of a Capacity in which we are all invited to par-
> ticipate. Undoubtedly, faith in the historical revelations of a living
> God ordained the book, but its philosophy, its metaphysics may be
> considered in themselves and figure in a history of philosophy, with-
> out automatically requiring adhesion. . . . As soon as an existential
> philosophy existed in the world, even if only in embryo and even if it
> was believed to be secular, it did nothing else except to turn like a
> moth around that philosophy. . . . Whether or not it so desired, it was
> the daughter or relative of prophetic thought, of the existential
> thought of Kafka. Whether or not it so desired, it was not Athenian
> either, but a daughter of the thought of Genesis, the existential
> thought of Nietzsche. . . . "

This was Fondane's original Jewish contribution to philosophical
thought before the Second World War. With regard to Fondane's Jewish
contribution to the literature of that period, although it was less original, it
was expressed in a significant manner in the novel *Ulysse* and in the collection of poems *Titanic*. These titles in themselves are enough to indicate
that these poems are associated with the theme of wandering, with which
Fondane identified to such a degree as to sign certain poems with the
pseudonym Isaac Laquedem, one of the names of the Wandering Jew in
French popular legend.

From the Exodus to the Burning Bush

But how could such an authentic person as Benjamin Fondane separate existence from essence, life from thought? In 1934 he composed the essential
parts, strangely prophetic in character, of *L'Exode, Super Flumina Babylonis*. This poem was at once an anticipation of and a commentary upon the
ten years in which it still remained to him to pursue his earthly path—a
path in the course of which the Bible, from being the Book, even though
written with a capital letter, now suddenly flared up like a Burning Bush.
Composed from 1934 onwards, the poem was added to in 1940, and
then in 1942, and completed in the convoys and camps of deportation. A
witness has related that Fondane carried the poem, handwritten on little

pages, in a metal box hanging from his neck. "If I die, take it off and give it to the last survivor," he said to his fellow deportees. And, indeed, the box has been preserved, a relic of Auschwitz, just as Yitzhak Katznelson's *Song of the Last Jew* survived in the bottles in which the author hid it in the camp of Vittel before being deported to Auschwitz and as Emmanuel Ringelblum's *Diary* was preserved in the ruins of the Warsaw Ghetto where the author perished after having committed his testimony to a bottle concealed in the ground.

In its complete form, the poem is set within two series of stanzas, each of which has for its title one of the twenty-two letters of the Hebrew alphabet, transcribed into Latin spelling. Thus, whatever the orientation of the thought, which is often chaotic, and whatever the style of the language which is sometimes esoteric, sometimes brutal and erotic, the whole is bound, by apparent or invisible threads, to the sub-structure of Hebrew language and mysticism.

Isaac Laquedem, in the course of his long wanderings, had lost the use, the memory, the elements of this language. He admitted as much in those parts of the poem not written in 1934, but added between 1940 and 1942: a rhythmical Prologue in prose and the long poem *L'Exode* which gave its name to the collection as a whole.

It is here that the expression *teshuva* applies, although in this case it is a Return within the Jewish dwelling place; but this dwelling place had been shaken up to such a degree that someone living inside it had also been shattered and torn apart.

Torn apart in his condition as a man, as the Prologue says so feelingly—as a man who, while being Jewish, believed and felt himself to be the same as other human beings. Suddenly, the persecution of the Jews brought him up against the phenomenon of "and yet, nevertheless," the inescapable mark of a Jewish existence, which no longer has anything in common with normal human existence.

"And yet, no!," he says.

The "I" and the "you" have detached themselves from one another. The Jewish "I" is thrown back into the solitary oneness of its martyrdom, while the "you" continues peacefully to live its life. A breath of despair passes through this poem, as also a breath of redemption, but the redemption only accentuates the despair, for the "I" and the "you" will be reconciled only "when death will have done its work," when the "I" will be ground to nothing, reduced to a clump of nettles under the impact of the "you"—of that comprehensive "you," part of which has played the role of murderers, and others, of uncaring and unfeeling witnesses. Humanity will understand the Jewish destiny, the universal will accept the existence of the Unique, but only when it is too late:

It's to you that I speak, men of the Southern hemisphere,
Speaking to you as man to man
With the little in me that is still human
And the little of my voice that subsists in my throat.
My blood has been shed on my paths and may it, ah, may it
Cease to cry aloud for revenge!
The kill has been called, the beasts hunted down,
So let me address you with those same words
That once we could share:
So little is still intelligible!

A day must come, I'm sure, of slaked thirst
When we'll all be beyond memory, when death
Will have accomplished all its tasks of hatred.
I'll then be only a clump of nettles beneath
Your feet, but remember then that I once had
A face like your own and a mouth that could pray
Like yours. When dust entered my eye, or a dream,
My eye wept salt like yours and when
An unfriendly thorn scratched my skin
My blood that it drew was red as yours!
Yes, I was cruel, as cruel as you, but could still
Thirst for tenderness too, or else for power
Or for gold, pleasure or even pain.
Like you I could be evil or anxious,
Reliable in peace or drunken in victory
And haggard and stumbling when I felt frustrated.

Yes, I've been a man like all other men,
Fed on bread and dreams and despair. Ah, yes,
I've loved and wept and hated and suffered
And purchased flowers and sometimes failed too
To pay my rent. On Sundays I went
To the country, went fishing beneath God's gaze
After unreal fish, or swam in a stream
That sang among the reeds, and I ate french fries
In the evening. After that, well, after that
I went home and slept, weary, with my heart
Brimful with loneliness and self-pity
And pity for all mankind while I sought
In vain, while I sought on a woman's body
That impossible peace we had lost

In the dim past in a great orchard blossoming
In its heart with a Tree of Life. . . .

Like you, I read all the newspapers, the paperbacks,
And failed to understand the world at all
And failed ever to understand man too
Though I often happened to affirm
That I could.
And when death came, my death, perhaps,
I claimed I knew what it was, but in truth,
I can tell you now, in this very hour,
Death entered my wide-open staring eyes
That were surprised that they understood so little.
Have you understood it better than I?

And yet no, after all!
I was never a man like you.
You were not born as I was, on the roads.
Nobody ever cast your children into the sewers
Like kittens whose eyes are not yet open.
You have never wandered through cities pursued by police,
Have never known disaster at dawn
Or been deported in cattle cars,
Never known the bitter sobs of humiliation
When accused of a crime while the corpse was still lacking,
Never changed your name and even your face
So as no longer to bear a name that had become an insult
And a face into which all your fellow citizens
Had spat!

A day may yet come, I'm sure, when this poem
Will be found before your eyes. It demands
Nothing. Forget it, forget it. What is it?
Only a cry that can never fit into
A perfect poem: Was I left enough time to polish it?
But when you tread at last on this clump of nettles
That I once was, in some later century,
Long after the forgotten century when I lived,
Remember only that I was innocent
And that, like you, men and women of the future,
I once had a face like yours that was marked
By anger and pity and joy, in fact

Simply a human face and no more!

In Thy Fearful Nights of Wrath

If the Prologue, written in 1942, stated the problem in horizontal terms (the Jew and the man), the main poem, written on the roads during the collapse of France in June 1940, is entirely vertical. Fondane would not have been a Jew outside humanity in 1942 if he had not previously, from 1940, from the time that the swastika was unfurled over France, felt that the man who he then was was being sought out by God and isolated in his Jewish identity.

There is a succession of salient moments in this process of elevation of the horizontal to the vertical which is fascinating to follow.

When the rivers yielded, one after the other, to the German advance—the Meuse, the Somme, the Maine, the Loire—Fondane, in his distress, still felt bound, even if only "by death," to the French identity of all the men who, from all the four corners of the earth, had sought and found liberty in the land of the Rights of Man, now threatened by the anti-man and the denial of rights.

At that moment, there was a sudden rupture ("We left Paris behind us"), and from that time onwards, from the time of that rupture, there was an upsurge of Jewish uniqueness, the eternal memory which returned to the surface and imprinted itself upon the consciousness in order to dwell there permanently, banishing everything that was foreign to it—the memory of the psalm of hope and longing for Zion: "If I forget thee, O Jerusalem!"

Once this Paris-Jerusalem antithesis appeared, there was a blind struggle between everything which illustrated that antithesis: the landscape (the Seine and the Shiloah), the language (the French in which the poem is written and the Hebrew of the key phrase, the Shema, following the Jew from birth to death, accompanying his sunrises and his sunsets, and appearing here in a touching transcription in which the Hebrew sound *Ehod,* one, is rhymed with a French word, *ode*), pity and anger, repentance and return, concealment and truth, literature and reality.

One had prayer, the prayer of the lone Jew sought out by the lone God: "And Jacob was left alone, and there wrestled a man with him until the breaking of the day" (Genesis 32:25).

But now there was something unexpected. Instead of an identification, which would seem natural here, of the Jew Benjamin Fondane with his ancestor Jacob-Israel, he identified himself with Aaron: "Behold, I am Aaron." Not the Aaron of the Golden Calf but Aaron the High Priest of Yom Kippur, laying hold of the scapegoat with his strong hands and sending him out into the desert.

And it is as the officiating priest on Yom Kippur that Benjamin Fondane went down on his knees and wept and shouted the Shema . . . as all the Jews since the time of Sinai, since Aaron, everywhere, in all the synagogues of the world have done on Yom Kippur:

We left Paris behind us. Ah, if ever
I forget thee, O Jerusalem! . . . Now
You were a city no longer but an ancient eucharist,
A wafer of flesh and blood
Which remained over there, but which also dwelt
With us—in captivity, outrage,
Anxiety, offense and disgust.
Sweet river, O Shiloah!
O Seine! And thou, Paris, Wailing Wall
Left for afterwards
When Assyria, inflated like a huge bladder,
Would burst!
How many Jews on this earth, O Lord! Stiffnecked,
Thickheaded, no doubt they have forgotten Thee. Yes,
And yet we cried towards Thee. Dost Thou recall
The scapegoat, which Aaron's strong hand once
Held and sent forth into the desert, bearing
Our impurities? Behold, I am Aaron;
I fall on my knees and I weep and I cry
In a tongue I have forgot, but
Remember in Thy fearful nights of wrath:
Adonai elohenu, Adonai ehod!

Adonai elohenu, Adonai ehod!
Have pity, have pity on the land of France!
How lovely it is! Such as Thou hast created it
From nothingness, with Thy knowing and loving hands
With its noble vineyards, its cathedrals and
Its plough-horses and clear-spirited men!
Have pity, have pity, Lord
On this France which I have known in books,
Pure, and yet which sickens me, soiled and full of blood,
With stomach ripped in the undefiled heart of my ode—
Adonai elohenu, adonai ehod!
Thou knowest that when all will be stilled
On earth and in the heavens
We shall have forgotten Thee. Thou knowest, even now,
That even the secret memory of my prayer
Will fill me with shame. I shall resent Thy
Having heard it; I shall resent my
Having said it. As Thou knowest, I have other gods
Than Thee—secret, treacherous!
But here, on the roads, in disaster and in

Chaos, there is no other God. Thou art alone!
Terrible, Fiery, Merciful, Unique!

KARL WOLFSKEHL

The two volumes of the complete works of Karl Wolfskehl are an extraordinary psychological document. The predicament of the European and German Jew of the twentieth century is expressed there in a more poignant
manner than Heine was able to express that of the nineteenth-century Jew.
It was the writer himself who chose the texts which he hoped would give
posterity a true idea of his creative inspiration. He had just passed the age
of seventy-five, a period which coincided with the end of the Second World
War. Born, like Heine, in the Rhineland, in 1869, he was—again like
Heine—to die far from Germany, in exile, in 1948. His complete works
were published only in 1960, but we are to understand that they were bequeathed to us in that form, as I said, by Karl Wolfskehl himself.

Thus, they are not so much "complete works" as selected or, rather,
hand-picked works, sifted in the crucible of criteria unknown except to the
author. One should visualize this robust, proud old man, sure of his poetic
powers: What he was doing was not to make a choice but a judgment, and
the criterion of that judgment was a date—the fateful date of 1933, the
advent of the Third Reich, the beginning of the Shoa. All works previous to
that date were condemned by this writer to disappearance, or at least not to
appear in the spiritual legacy of the two volumes of his complete works.

The Germanic Fiefdom

This body of work previous to 1933 still exists. It has been published in
volumes which will continue to figure on the shelves of libraries. It is a
corpus of work which places Karl Wolfskehl among the outstanding poets
of the German symbolist school. He was one of the favorite disciples of
Stefan George, a demiurge who admitted only an elite into his circle which
was ready, like him, to express in an esoteric language an outlook in which
the Europe of Nietzsche cohabited with the Germany of Wagner and, already, the Messianism of a Führer—a key principle of which we shall never
know whether, in Stefan George's estimation, Hitler was the usurper or the
heir (George died in 1933).

In this circle of Stefan George, Karl Wolfskehl's work was marked by
its servility, a term which, in the sense in which we use it here, has nothing
pejorative about it. As used here, it indicates the condition of the serf
ennobled by the feudal relationship which binds him to his lord. The fiefdom of Karl Wolfskehl was one of the domains conceded by Stefan George
to his serfs: the epics of medieval Germanic mythology which Richard

Wagner had taken out of its lethargy in order to nourish the spiritual life of Germany nearly a century before. A son of the Rhineland, Karl Wolfskehl chose the cycle of the Nibelungen, full of the golden iridescence of the Rhine, recast it in a modern German idiom, and presented it together with his own poems, also cast in the spirit of the Rhine—a Germanic river, the last frontier of the Roman Empire, the cradle of Charlemagne's Europe, a special meeting place of the major ideas of the West.

It was a brilliant body of work. It was sincere. It reflected the organic cohesion of this serf of a European Germany in which his Jewish origins had their place, limited but undeniable. For Karl Wolfskehl believed that his ancestors had belonged to the Kalonymos family, Jewish poets and thinkers who had come from Italy to the Rhineland in those Middle Ages whose spoken language he, their distant descendant, was now restoring to life. It was an illustration of the continuous coexistence of the Jewish condition and of Germanic culture, the symbol of a symbiosis which it seemed that nothing would ever cast doubt on or put in question.

And it was this body of work which Karl Wolfskehl as an old man now destroyed, throwing the scraps into the wastepaper basket and leaving nothing in his legacy but the works written after 1933.

These works contradicted the former ones from beginning to end. These works were founded on an integral Judaism: poems, each verse, each word of which was inspired exclusively by Jewish tradition. Only the style remains German, although often many terms of the Judeo-German dialect and Hebrew words find their way into it. On one occasion, even the title of a collection of poems was Hebrew, taken from the Bible (Hosea 4:7): *Kalon Becavod Namir* (We Shall Replace Shame With Honor).

The Flight to the Antipodes

This leap from a universally oriented work to a work of purely Jewish significance in itself constitutes a striking act of *teshuva*, but Wolfskehl's deliberate rejection of his work previous to his *teshuva* reveals a horizontal drama which ought not to obscure the vertical aspect of the *teshuva*.

The case of Karl Wolfskehl can, in effect, be interpreted as an extreme example of the horizontal relationship between the Jews and Germany. If he is but rarely referred to, that is because Wolfskehl's life and work are not sufficiently known. Scholem does not mention his name even once, yet he could have referred to him as a typical example of what he called the "myth of the Judeo-German dialogue." Indeed, by his *teshuva*, Wolfskehl acknowledged and expressed the fact that the Judeo-German symbiosis was only an illusion, a phantom, a mirage.

From the first weeks of the advent of the Third Reich and the adoption of the swastika as the German national emblem, he felt that something had unquestionably been broken. He left Germany, not furtively but most demonstratively, calling, in the poems he wrote at that time, on his co-religionists and non-Jewish compatriots to act in the same way as he and choose exile. But not a land of exile where one's gaze may still rest on Germany. He did not go to Switzerland or Italy; he did not go to Palestine either—it was still too close to Europe. He chose New Zealand, the antip-odes. In this way he wished to stress his total uprooting from what had proved to be a bitter illusion.

He preserved this distance until his death in New Zealand, where he asked to be buried. From 1945 onwards he could have returned to Germany, which friends invited him to come back to, Arnold Zweig, Ernst Bloch, Theodor Adorno, his comrades-in-arms from before 1933, did indeed go back. In a poignant poem in the form of a diptych, *An die Deutschen* (1946), which he intended as his Song of Farewell (*Abgesang*), Karl Wolf-skehl explained the reason for his rupture.

A first panel evoked the former Judeo-German intimacy, introducing each stanza with the theme of community—community of language, of po-etic creation, of civic life, of dreams, of the rhythm of daily existence. . . . But the second panel, cast in one piece, opened with an acknowledgment of a rupture, now eternal: *Losgebrochen!* Something had definitely snapped in the relationship between the Jew and Germany. Their paths could no longer converge: Each had to go his own way.

But to stop here would be to divest the drama of Karl Wolfskehl of its main significance. The divergence of paths is not only horizontal. And the interpreters (especially German) of Wolfskehl's thought who wish to con-centrate everything on this instant of rupture in which, they say, despite everything, the reality of a past of symbiosis and coexistence contains the promise of a reconciliation in the future—these interpreters curtail Wolf-skehl's spiritual adventure (in which—and this, too, is symptomatic—they wish at all costs to perceive traces of Christianity which are entirely non-existent).

The Irruption of the Voice: The Fiefdom of God

For the Jew Karl Wolfskehl, to break with Germany was not only to break with a certain past because today there had been a betrayal on the part of that same Germany. The betrayal was that the Jew Karl Wolfskehl had been able, for so many long years of his life, to imagine that the coexistence of Germany and the Jews, of Europe and the Jews, of humanity and the Jews was possible without God being present in that coexistence. When his an-cestor Kalonymos, in the Middle Ages, poured Rhenish wine into his gob-let, it was for the purpose of performing the rites of the Kiddush and the Havdalah of the Sabbath and not in order to celebrate the Rhine as a source of spiritual nourishment. Now, once again, God demanded his share, but the time that had been wasted in the interim now required that this share should be absolute, all-embracing. There could no longer be any fiefdom outside that of God.

The silence was broken. The Voice Speaks, *Die Stimme spricht:* That was the title of the first collection, published hastily in 1933 and followed by others, including *The Song of Exile* and a tetralogy, *Job or the Four Mirrors.*

Each of these titles had some particular significance. The Exile, for instance, was not a running away, but a perpetual questioning of a settled existence. If one asks where one should go, the answer is that it hardly matters. What matters is to escape the servitude of human values in order to serve exclusively the values of the Absolute. That was one of the reasons why, despite Karl Wolfskehl's very strong theoretical support of Zionism, and despite the enthusiasm with which he hailed the restoration of the State of Israel in the very year in which he died, he nevertheless did not choose Palestine, still too much part of human civilization, as his place of exile. He wanted to be alone with God. He identified his fate with that of Job, to whom he devoted his tetralogy which was as hermetic as it was fascinating, and in which one progressed in a mysterious, yet irrevocable manner from Job-Israel to Job-Samson and then to Job-Nabi and finally to Job-Messiah.

The Four Mirrors of Job

Job-Israel represents the sufferings of the Suffering Servant, the fate of Jewish tears which constitute the "harsh wine of the soul." Job-Samson represents the Jew leaping up to destroy the idols, ideologies, and ideas manufactured by the "right- (and wrong) thinking" Europe of the Philistines who create Jewish suffering or look on impassive or indifferent to that suffering.

Job-Nabi is prophetic awakening, the Voice of God which emerges from the Hidden Face. One had thought that God was absent, or, rather, the philosopher of eternal recurrence, Nietzsche, had created the myth of the death of God, and yet here the Living God lives again, not only as such but in the form of the only true eternal recurrence which is the Return of God in history.

For Job-Messiah (to take the last figure) is not Job going towards God but God coming towards Job. As Wolfskehl saw it, the springboard of Messianism lay in Job himself, in the fact that he is addressed in the second person—that "thou" which passes through the history of the Jewish people, its tradition, and its continuity in light and shade until one finally reaches that Messiah who cannot be anything else than Thou:

Who, if not Thou?
When, if not today?
Where, if not right here?

This variation of a celebrated saying from the *Pirkei Avot* in the Talmud is the legend of the last mirror in which Wolfskehl reveals Job's reflection, the mirror in which, at the end, there takes place the miracle of the beginning. The "Thou" regains its position, discovers its Covenant with the Him and confirms this Covenant whereby Presence and Absence, Eternity and Timelessness, Existence and Sacrifice indissolubly reconcile the irreconcilable:

Job—is Thou—the Messiah is Thou.
Who?—HIM—YOU.

The Voice Speaks

So, one had this proud solitude of Wolfskehl in his refuge of New Zealand, without friends, without enemies, without confidants, without doubters. In the company of a devoted secretary, Margot Ruben, who related to me the heroism of this deliberate solitude taken upon himself as a redemptive act. At the antipodes of any trace of human civilization but in alliance with God, for God broke this proud solitude and made it even prouder with His lofty call. At the close of his short collection *Job or The Four Mirrors*, which appeared only after Wolfskehl's death, one is brought back to his first collection as a *ba'al teshuva*, *The Voice Speaks:*

The Voice speaks: Where art thou? The penetrating Jewish
  ontological question.
The Voice speaks: On the Great Day of the Sabbath.
The Voice speaks: At the Seder.
The Voice speaks: Through Edom and Amalek.
The Voice speaks: We are persecuted by everything, and yet we are
  still there!
The Voice speaks: *Kalon Becavod Namir* (We Shall Replace Shame
  With Honor).

The whole range of the "meta" resounds in the Voice.

This is the Voice of the divine "nevertheless," of God's "and for all that"—the Voice of the God who never wearies nor ever allows respite, even if the Jew steals away. It is the Voice of the "meta" which finds its culmination in the "meta" of the "meta," the day of the Great Return, Yom Kippur:

The Voice Speaks to Israel on Yom Hakippurim

Yes, I shall walk again
—Although your sloth abounds—
The garden of My word
Which holiness surrounds.

And I shall seek again
—Though not a tear you knew—
The curse begot the cure,
Because I wept for you.

And I shall come again
—Although you would not stand—
To you, the scattered hosts,
Who long have slipped my hand.

And I shall weave again
—Although you have not fulled—
My web of vines. The weeds
Among the stones are pulled.

And I shall call again
—Although you slacked and dozed—
My casks will clear the wine,
I guard the cellar close.

And I shall sign again
—Although you failed to greet—
Until the last of bonds
Fall from your head and feet.

And I shall lead again
—Though laxly you withdrew—
Not one of all my gates
Shall be denied to you.

And I shall storm again
—Although you did not surge—
Inside and out the old-
New gales will blast and scourge . . .

Shall bless again, again,

That I vowed you to Me,
Until we meet at last,
Whole in eternity.

Do you know, do you know what is here being born?
Do you know the meaning of Kippur?
Do you know who has kept watch over you
From dawn, early in the morning and late at night?

Do you know when He forgets you?
Do you know when He is there, at the moment of Kippur?

Do you know who sends forth the cry of Kippur,
Who traces for you the path, the only one,
Leading unswervingly to an inevitable Covenant?

Do you know what Yom Kippur is for?
Do you know who silently traces and germinates
His furrows in the universe?
The impenetrable, the ineffable?
Do you know? Why do you shed tears?

The "Old-new Gales"

Here we should mention a remarkable detail. The collection *The Voice Speaks* went into two successive editions: one of October 1933 and the other of winter 1934. There was a space of three months between the two editions, which were identical in every respect, except that the poem "The Voice Speaks To Israel On Yom Hakippurim" is missing in the first edition. It was as though the poet, having lived through Yom Kippur of October 1933, suddenly felt that something in the call of the Voice was lacking— the call of Yom Kippur. Like a peasant retracing his steps in order to gather a forgotten sheaf of corn, Wolfskehl hastened to repair the omission, and in the winter of 1934 the collection was republished in a new edition containing this one call, this one cry which the poet had forgotten.

It is impossible for us today, at forty years' distance and a few years after the Yom Kippur War, to read these two versions of the same poem without feeling that we are confronted with a prophetic intuition on Wolfskehl's part of the importance of the essential relationship between the very fact of Yom Kippur and the eternal significance of the destiny of the Jewish people. It is as if the poet were still addressing us through his poem, as if to say: "Do not make the same mistake as I did! Do not imagine that you can close your eyes to that day which is called Yom Kippur. If there really is a Voice which speaks to Israel, you can only understand its significance (assuming that that voice has a significance) through the call which that Voice makes to you on Yom Kippur.''

Thus the *ba'al teshuva* Karl Wolfskehl expressed, through a belated inspiration whose trace is preserved for us in the two editions of his collection, the central position of Yom Kippur in the Jew's personal and collective destiny—the individual destiny of the *ba'al teshuva* in all periods, and that of the whole of Israel when, at the moment of collective *teshuva,* on October 6, 1973, a war broke out which has entered history under the name of the Yom Kippur War.

9

The Returners from Marxism

THE JEWS OF THE AWAKENING

Social revolt was born in the Bible. It was the Jewish prophets, headed by Moses, who created it and gave it to humanity.

Why, then, this mysterious phenomenon of a situation that repeated itself after a period of 128 years? Namely, that the two great revolutions of modern times, the French Revolution of 1789 and the Russian Revolution of 1917—revolutions to which the Jews gave the best of themselves—repaid the Jews for their enthusiasm with the opposite requirement—they put their Jewish souls into these revolutions, but they were first required to divest themselves of them! It was only by means of this divestment that the Jewish contribution was accepted by their non-Jewish comrades-in-arms.

But this first sacrifice, agreed to by the Jews themselves, was not considered sufficient. A second one was added, demanded by the non-Jewish revolutionaries: the rejection of the Jews from the new society founded by the revolution.

Thus the tragedy of European Judaism, a victim far removed of the illusion of 1789, unfolded before our eyes together with the tragedy of Russian Judaism, a victim closer at hand of the mirage of 1917. Many cases of "returning" in this book are characteristic of the situation experienced by the Jews of Europe who believed—excessively—in the assimilation proposed by the Revolution of 1789. We could devote a whole book to the "returning" of the Jews of the USSR, to the awakening of the third generation, to those courageous men in whom the sparks, smothered by their own fathers and sometimes by themselves, suddenly flared up once more. But this is taking place at the very moment when we are writing these lines. I do not wish to run the risk of being ungrateful to some and forgetting others. . . . Let us therefore take the measure of this event through three characteristic cases of men who are no longer living but who form part of the body of these Jews of the Awakening.

RUTENBERG, STEINBERG: THE FIGHTERS OF THE OCTOBER REVOLUTION

Petrograd, October 25, 1917. The Bolsheviks had begun the attack upon the Winter Palace. This was the final, victorious phase of the ultra-red revolution. The infra-red revolution of February—that of the Mensheviks and particles of moderate groups—had faded into oblivion. Its leader, Kerensky, had already taken flight and others, like him, had left the scene of combat. None of his associates were willing to exert power now that power had become only nominal: none, except, of course—as always—a Jew. That terrifying fidelity of the Jews! This Jew, who was the governor of the capital, was ready to enter the frail canoe of the provisional government of the new Russia and simultaneously to defend Petrograd, the Winter Palace, and the country of the "good" red revolution against the disloyal attack of the forces of the "bad" revolution, to defend them to the end at his command post, without any troops to command—the symbol of socialist liberty! To defend them to the point of sacrifice, to the point of death. This Jew—alone, of course, as always—this solitary and abandoned Jew was called Piotr Rutenberg.

In the attacking party, in the overpowering shadow of the great leader Lenin, there were masses of Jews: old Bolsheviks, but also those who had rallied in recent weeks. One of them had for a long time been a Menshevik. Now he led the soldiers who directed their arms against the Winter Palace and were to take it under his direction. In the immediate future, he was to command them on the first and fiercest battlefields of Bolshevik Soviet Russia. This Jew, born Leo Bronstein, was Trotsky.

More inconspicuous, but very close to Lenin and waiting excitedly for the triumph of his cause—one of the Jews who would make important contributions to the new political order—was a social revolutionary, a moderate who had come around to the Bolsheviks. He was to become Commissar of Justice in the first Supreme Soviet following the victory of October. This Jew was called Itshak Steinberg.

So you had Trotsky and Steinberg versus Rutenberg. It was an example of the fratricidal combat waged by so many Jews from August 1, 1914, onwards. But what concerns us here is not their confrontation but the erosion of the constituent elements of the universe of these three men. None of the three was to remain in Soviet Russia beyond the time of Lenin, but their break and their new orientation was to take place, for each of the three, in totally differing conditions.

It is useless to give a place of importance in this book to Trotsky. Where history is concerned, he has his place assured among the anti-Jewish Jews, the representatives of self-hatred. Long after his break with Russia,

Trotsky got angry when a journalist asked him whether his revolutionary fervor did not owe something to his Jewish atavism, to the hopes of the prophets of Israel: "No, no! Not Yid, not Yid!," he answered. A journalist told Arnold Mandel that he held on a leash a great wolfhound and had himself pulled forward by the animal, who showed his teeth. But Trotsky's teeth have bitten into history far beyond the chance circumstance of his Jewish birth, and it is not to an analysis of the portion of Judaism in Trotskyism, neo-Trotskyism, or Maoist Trotskyism that this book is devoted.

On the other hand, this *is* the place to analyze the Rutenberg-Steinberg polarity, which expressed itself in the form of a political contradiction within the great socialist family in October 1917 and later as another form of contradiction within the great Jewish family, for these two socialist-communists, over and above their divergences in the struggle for the victory of the proletariat, were brothers in the lucidity and pride of their attitude to their Jewish origins. It was from these that they both derived a naive and boundless idealism which they placed at the service of the Marxist revolution; and then, when that revolution betrayed their ideals, they returned to the Jewish people whose message had nurtured them. They thus returned to a path they had traveled long before their engagement in the social struggle which led first to the Russian Revolution and then envisaged the transformation of the world. It was this same transformation which they were now about to attempt as survivors of Marxism, but in transferring their sphere of activity to the people which had given birth to Marx and to their own Marxism—the Jewish people, the people of the Bible and the prophetic revolt, and that also of the nineteenth-century Russian *shtetl* where they had gained their human culture. If they both turned their backs on Marxism, however, their gaze turned towards a form of Judaism which in either case was radically different. Piotr became Pinhas, but Itshak . . . remained Itshak. It is in this mutation of the first name of one of them and the continuity of the first name of the other that the difference between their forms of return is indicated.

For Rutenberg, the change from Piotr to Pinhas represented more than a tension between Russian and Jewish identity in one and the same soul. Rutenberg was only Russian, he only wanted to be Russian when he served the Revolution; he was purely Jewish, he only wanted to be Jewish, when he served Zionism. We should remember that the tension was not a linear one. The point of rupture between Piotr and Pinhas was not limited to the series of events in Rutenberg's life which took place in quick succession between November 1917 and November 1919: his arrest in the Winter Palace, his six months in prison, his release, his flight from Bolshevist Moscow to Kiev which had become the briefly independent capital of his native Ukraine, his move to Odessa and his participation in an equally ephemeral "white" government supported by France (Weygand!), and finally his embarkation for Palestine by the Odessa-Jaffa sea route which had been taken by his fellow Zionists at the end of the nineteenth century and which would still be used by the fellow Zionists fleeing Soviet Russia whom Pinhas Reutenberg was to receive in Palestine from November 1919 onwards.

THE PIOTR-PINHAS ADVENTURE

For the fact was that Pinhas Rutenberg, born in 1879, had been a Zionist in his youth, but at the turn of the century the socialist revolution fascinated him, took hold of him, and made him a Russian underground fighter—Piotr—leaving the cellars in which plots were hatched only for the prisons of the Czar. The decisive year 1905 projected him onto the forefront of history: One "Red Sunday" the Jew Piotr Rutenberg walked side by side with the priest Gapon in an advance on the Winter Palace in St. Petersburg. This was the first high point of his revolutionary career, and also his first setback. He had to accept the facts which sullied the purity of his ideals: Brother Gapon was only an agent provocateur in the pay of the Czarist police! The storm in Piotr's brain lasted nearly a year. Despite the evidence, he helped Gapon to get away, but, compelled by the evidence, he was entrusted with Gapon's execution. Betrayed by Gapon, by his comrades, and by his ideals, Piotr left Russia in 1907. A qualified engineer of the Technological Institute of St. Petersburg and a specialist in problems of irrigation, he placed his talents at the service of Italy which received him as an émigré, and there, no longer dealing with the ideal but with reality, but nevertheless longing for an alternative ideal, he rediscovered the Zionism of his youth. Piotr once again became Pinhas, so much so that, when war broke out in August 1914, he suddenly left Italy, which was indifferent to Zionist aspirations, and went to London where the Weizmann-Sokolov-Ahad Ha'am group, which was to wage the struggle that would lead to the Balfour Declaration of November 1917, was already being formed.

Rutenberg was so enthusiastic about the attempt to turn the Zionist ideal into a reality that he advocated the formation of a Jewish army for the liberation of Palestine, and hence struck up a friendship with Vladimir Jabotinsky (that "man of the right"!) and traveled to America to recruit volunteers and to present the American leaders with the Zionist demands to be made at the Peace Conference which would one day undoubtedly be held at the end of the war. Among these demands was a vast project for the irrigation of Palestine: the resurrection of the Jewish soil and the Jewish people at a single bound. He published a résumé of his vision in which technical genius went hand-in-hand with enthusiasm of the spirit under the title: *The National Resurrection of the Jewish People,* signing it Pinhas Ben-Ami (Pinhas Son-of-my-People). This was the first high point of Rutenberg's

Zionist career. He was now, to all appearances, fully a Son-of-his-People in the Zionistic sense of this glowing biblical term.

SON OF MOTHER RUSSIA

But even stronger than Zionism was the Revolution. As soon as the first cracks in the Czar's empire appeared at the beginning of 1917, the old dream awakened in the hearts of the émigrés of 1905. From the four corners of their exile they hastened towards Russia, and this call of the siren also reached the very heart of Pinhas Ben-Ami, revolutionary Son of Mother Russia. Rutenberg quickly left London, breaking his connection with the Zionist struggle in order to renew his links with the socialist struggle.

Bitter ironies of this adventure of a hopeless lover of a revolution which deceived him at every turn! When the Balfour Declaration, for whose pronouncement Pinhas Rutenberg had worked so hard, and which had been received with such enthusiasm by his Zionist colleagues throughout the world (and even by some in Russia, in Odessa, which the revolution had not yet reached) was issued in London in November 1917, Rutenberg, as we have seen, was now only the miserable Piotr, vanquished in the Winter Palace by a revolution more violent than his own, disappointed of the fruits of the struggle which, from February onwards, he had waged together with Kerensky. And on February 27th, 1919, when Weizmann, Sokolov, Ussishkin, Silvain Lévi, and André Spire presented the "blue-white" Zionist demands, to which Pinhas Rutenberg had made such a precious technical and economic contribution, at the Peace Conference, Piotr Rutenberg was helping to "govern" Odessa under a white and tricolored flag.

But, as we said, the break came quite soon, and Piotr, now once again Pinhas Ben-Ami, was already in Palestine when the Zionist "old-timers" of Odessa were in turn allowed to leave Soviet Russia for Palestine.

SON OF MY PEOPLE ISRAEL

Pinhas Rutenberg's work in Palestine from his *aliyah* in 1919 to his death in 1942 was an admirable sequel: a brilliant synthesis of technical achievement and politics and a desperate endeavor to construct the Jewish National Home on the incredible basis of a unity between the most various and the most opposing tendencies. He achieved the electrification and, through that very fact, the industrialization of Palestine, at the same time as being president of the Va'ad Leumi, the "Jewish government," in years of crisis—in 1929 (the economic crisis) and 1939 (beginning of the Second World War and the *Shoa*). He was at the head of the Haganah in Tel Aviv during the Arab disturbances of 1921 and later joined Magnes in his fantastic search for an understanding between Jews and Arabs. For a certain length of time, he succeeded in reconciling the irreconcilable: Ben-Gurion and Jabotinsky. He was the arbitrator to whom one had recourse when inter-human relations were short-circuited. He restored contacts and re-established currents in the political, cultural, and moral sphere with as much skill and spirit of sacrifice as in the physical sphere. In 1942, at the height of the *Shoa*, he bequeathed, before dying, his message of unity to Jewish youth, investing its potential for the future with all the tumultuous experience of his own past. The fact that his house on Mount Carmel has become a Youth Center sums up the significance of Pinhas Rutenberg's "return." It was a return to his own Zionist youth, but enriched with the revolutionary tensions which had shaken him without destroying him, which had dazzled him without blinding him, and which confirmed what they appeared to invalidate—the prophetically revolutionary potential of the Jewish Zionist idea.

EMBARKED UPON THE PHANTOM SHIP OF LIBERTY

Should one, in order to pinpoint the revolutionary tensions of Itshak Steinberg, simply erase the adjective "Zionist," and limit oneself to observing that he conceivably joins Rutenberg in taking upon himself the prophetically revolutionary potential of the *Jewish* idea? That would be to mutilate Itshak Steinberg's Jewish personality. In the case of this Jew, from the cradle to the grave, religion, revolution, and nationalism were one and the same thing. In one of its facets, his Jewish nationalism embraced the Zionist ideal, the positive cognizance of what he himself called "the romantic and magnetic power of the ancient Jewish fatherland, Palestine." Like Rutenberg, moreover, he paradoxically felt himself to be closer to Jabotinsky than to Weizmann. In Russia he was the disciple of Zalman Rabinkov, and linked by friendship—a friendship which was never to fail—with another of Rabinkov's disciples who was later to become the third president of the State of Israel, Zalman Shazar.

But his nationalism was inspired by a mightier and even more magnetic idea than that of the biblical Eretz Israel: the lofty, vertiginous, inaccessible, and utopian idea of Liberty. It was this idea which transcended the revolutionary Marxism of Steinberg, provoking his break with Soviet Russia and the communist cause with which he had long identified himself. In all this, throughout the ruptures and changes, there was a fundamental, solid, unbreakable fidelity, the backbone of Itshak Steinberg's life and thought. Jewish religious fidelity, the scrupulous observance of the commandments of the Torah, a simple, natural, spontaneous "orthodoxy," submission to kashrut, prayer, the Sabbath, the festivals—all that the Zionist, Marxist, emancipated Jews had begun to throw overboard, and which Itshak Steinberg was careful to carry with him in his existential embarkation on a ship on which fate had allotted him the role now of a captain, now of a stowaway. This ship was called the phantom ship of Liberty.

JEWISH PRAYER AT THE HEART OF THE SUPREME SOVIET

It was this religious orthodoxy which enabled Steinberg to avoid altering his first name. Throughout the labyrinth of "befores" and "afters" of his eventful life, he remained Itshak with a continuity whose key point was undoubtedly the three months (from December 1917 to March 1918) when Itshak Steinberg was Commissar for Justice in the first Supreme Soviet of the new Union of Soviet Socialist Republics. The meetings of the Supreme Soviet were often held at Lenin's, in his room at the Smolny, in an atmosphere which Steinberg was later to characterize as "idyllic." There is a photograph showing all the Bolsheviks and social revolutionaries dressed in bourgeois clothes, sitting around a samovar. Steinberg is right next to Lenin and Trotsky. One can sense, from the tension in the faces, how important and decisive were the problems under consideration, how violent and heated the discussions were. What the photo does not show, however, but trustworthy witnesses have heard, or claimed to hear, is a word of Lenin's which relaxed the atmosphere and allowed everyone to breathe for a few minutes. Lenin turned to Steinberg. Lenin had just looked at his watch: Evening was drawing near. "Itshak," he said, "have you prayed *minha* yet? Go quickly to your usual place, or it will be too late!" And even if this is only an anecdote, amplified by hearsay, it provides a lively portrait of the two polarities of the Jewish personality of Itshak Steinberg: his religious orthodoxy and his faith in liberty.

LIBERTY GRAVEN IN THE LAW . . .

Both polarities simultaneously drew him away from the Russian Revolution, for the observance of the Torah, for Steinberg, was simply a form of liberty. Did not rabbinical tradition teach that what was graven (*harut*) on the Tablets of the Law was precisely liberty (*herut*)? And, at a deeper level, do not the Bible and the Talmud identify the idea of liberty with that of justice? It was in the name of the Jewish concept of justice—the biblical *tsedek*—that Steinberg threw himself as a student into the struggles which led up to the failed revolution of 1905. There was a period of underground fighting and prisons and a flight to Germany, where he wrote his doctoral thesis on a revealing subject: *Criminal Law in the Talmud.* The general character of his early career resembles that of Rutenberg, but when these two men were both in Russia in 1917, they were to be found in opposite

camps. Steinberg chose the social revolutionary stream. It was intermediate
between the Mensheviks and Bolsheviks, but soon divided into a right wing
which rallied to the government of Kerensky and a left wing which joined
Lenin. Steinberg was one of the leaders of this left wing, because in his
opinion, the Jewish ideals of liberty and justice could only triumph through
a total revolution. It was this absoluteness of his revolutionary conception
which had caused him to be rejected by the "bourgeois" lawyer Grusen-
berg from the bar when he had sought to join the defense at the time of the
Beilis affair in 1913, just as his religious convictions had from the beginning opposed him to the Bund. The compromise between the Bund and
Kerensky was one more reason to put himself resolutely on the side of
Lenin.

. . . AND JUSTICE AS WELL

On the side of Lenin, his October revolution and his vision of liberty, but
not of Bolshevism. On the side of the Smolny, with its violent but free
discussions, but not the "invisible catacombs" of the Kremlin. Between the
violence inherent in any revolution and non-violence, ideal expression of
liberty, Steinberg sought a middle way. His position as Commissar of Justice made it clear to him: The limit of violence is terror. The example of the
French Revolution reminded the Russian Revolution how easy and dangerous it is to pass from violence to terror.

As in 1793, moreover, the issue was not a theoretical one. The battle
against the extension of violence into terror had to be fought in the heat of
action, in the feverish atmosphere of the war against Germany on the western frontier and the relentless search for "counter-revolutionaries" within
the country. Still starker than the confrontation of the Girondins and la
Montagne was that between the social revolutionaries and the Bolsheviks.
In three months, as Steinberg said, one "passed from idyll to tragedy."
Lenin's invitation to Steinberg to go and pray Minha, even if it is a fiction,
reflects the idyllic atmosphere of the beginnings. It was not so much a
matter of tolerance towards Steinberg's naive and inoffensive religious pre-
occupations (the Jew Trotsky was the only one of the Soviet leaders to
make fun of them) as of a few minutes' respite in which, unknown to his
Commissar of Justice, immersed in heavenly things, Lenin handed over a
few heads of counter-revolutionaries to Dzerzhinsky, the ruthless head of
the Cheka (secret police). Steinberg had already risen up in opposition to
the very principle of the death sentence, previously condemned by Lenin
also but now reintroduced under the compulsion of historical necessity. At
least the Cheka remained juridically subordinate to the Commissariat for
Justice, and for a few weeks Steinberg had the illusion that no condemna-
tion could be made outside the binding framework of the law—that law for

which he vouched and which enabled him to save a large number of suspects from death. But, in February 1918, one had to recognize the facts. The Terror had triumphed and had legally set itself up at the very heart of the revolution: the Cheka was made independent of the Commissariat of Justice. Autonomous, it would henceforth practice its own brand of justice, which no longer had anything in common with biblical justice. It was even the exact antithesis of it.

Steinberg resigned. They let him leave, only too happy to be rid of his embarrassing and restricting stipulations. Soon, the way was opened up for Stalin.

THE NON-PROMISED LAND OF UTOPIA

Steinberg now left Russia, from whence he carried away the rich symbol of his forename Itshak, preserved intact through the most terrible of disappointments. Henceforth, his rupture with the socialist revolution was complete. He made a return, also complete, to pure Judaism, but whereas, within Judaism, Rutenberg at this same period chose the path of Zionism, Steinberg, for his part, chose territorialism. During the long years of the inter-war period, during the Shoa, after the Shoa, just before the creation of the State of Israel, and during the first ten years of Israel, Steinberg took refuge first in Germany, then in England, and finally in the United States, where he died in 1957. He fought with stubborn persistence and quixotic idealism in the Freeland political movement which sought to assure the Jewish people a home in a "non-promised land"—in Australia, in Surinam . . . or, rather—and this is the fundamental principle of Itshak Steinberg's adventure—in the land of Utopia. Without flinching before difficulties, without recoiling on account of the dangers which his actions and writings (pamphlets, a novel, autobiographical narratives) constituted for the recognition and the existence of the State of Israel, Itshak Steinberg rejected that State precisely because it *was* a State. Statehood, the necessity for compromise entailed by a state, the dialectical inflection of justice towards raison d'etat—everything he had fought against in his three months of power in the Soviet Union—Steinberg desperately wanted to spare the Jewish people. It was in the midst of a national community other than its own, which would take upon itself, in its stead, the inevitable compromises of state politics, that the Jewish people, in Steinberg's conception, was to live, in full liberty, but also in the full, untarnished observance of biblical and Talmudic principles of justice. Is not the Bible the great insurrectionist against authority? (See the rejection of royalty by the prophet Samuel.) Was not the Talmud the product of a people who had lived without the apparatus of statehood, in cultural autonomy within the Roman, Persian, Parthian, and Arab empires?

His fidelity to the imperatives of the Bible taken to the point of the meta-human and the unattainable made him renounce Zionism and its human components.

A dreamer at the helm of a phantom ship, he sought to be so closely bound to the principles of Justice and Liberty consecrated by the Covenant of Sinai that he lost its human dimensions, and because he attempted to push his Judaism too high, too far, he lost its sense of the experiential and of the realizable on earth.

10

The Pilgrim of Hope: Ernst Bloch

GENESIS IS AT THE END

Genesis is not at the beginning: It is at the end. . . . When man will have found the roots of his being, those which will allow him to transform and to transcend what is given, then something will be born in the world which everyone perceives in the radiance of his youth and where no one has ever been: *Heimat,* a Homeland . . .

A strange conclusion to Ernst Bloch's book cum rock-and-sledgehammer, *The Principle of Hope.* Strange through the breath of transcendence with which this masterwork of a twentieth-century Marxist ends, and strange through its points of correspondence with the divergent experiences of the two Jewish Marxists whose stories we have just touched on, bringing one, Pinhas Rutenberg, to the finally regained Homeland, Eretz Israel, and taking the other, Itshak Steinberg, towards the mirage of an undiscoverable country. Between them is Ernst Bloch, midway between the fleeting horizon of the ideal undiscoverable country and the already lived experience of the ingenuous country of infancy.

Would it be a forced interpretation of Bloch's thought to see in this Homeland situated in the past the Jewish area in the life of Ernst Bloch? An area concerning which he expressed himself in terms which are sometimes cautious, over-cautious, but for which he found, from the very inception of his work, a symbol which, in the self-containedness of its significance, marks an end rather than a beginning: "Genesis which is not at the beginning but at the end." This intensely Jewish symbol I too will reveal, but only at the end of this excursion with Ernst Bloch, for one should not present the jewel in the crown without first having given an account of the sovereign who wears it.

THE COUNTERPOINT OF
A JEWISH MELODY

Bloch's break with the Marxist establishment was spectacular. It was a by-product of Budapest 1956, and was geographically expressed by the professor's move from the University of Leipzig in East Germany to the University of Tübingen in West Germany. But, even before 1956, Soviet Russia was never for Ernst Bloch a Homeland. If any proof was needed, it was his voluntary exile in the time of the Third Reich, not in the Union of Soviet Socialist Republics, but in the United States. Could the State of Israel have been the Homeland of Ernst Bloch? If it is remarkable that in 1967, during the Six-Day War, detaching himself from leftists and communists of all kinds, he descended into the streets of Tübingen in order to proclaim his solidarity with the endangered Jewish state, that does not obviate the great and deliberate distance he takes from the state in all his works on ideological grounds. But neither, like Itshak Steinberg, did he search for a "Homeland" in some sheltered territory. The challenge he confronted was something he demanded for every man and not only for the Jew: To face directly, full on, the paradox of Utopia, the only Homeland for which man exists but into which, however, he cannot yet— *noch nicht*—enter. This is not the existential Nebo, for man does not *die* facing this elusive utopia: He lives facing it. It is . . . what is it, then? Prometheus chained on his rock? Jesus nailed to his cross? The Greek or Christian Passion with its endless potential of eternity as an image of history chained or nailed by Karl Marx on the rock or cross of determinism?

At times, the utopian Marxism of Ernst Bloch does have recourse to this Greek or Christian terminology, to myths and symbols in which critics have a fine time determining the "humanism" or the "Christianizing tendency" in the Marxism of Ernst Bloch.

And why not Freudian analysis? Structural exegesis? Dodecaphonic tonalities? In the gigantic labyrinth of the thought of Ernst Bloch, everything, in fact, can be found. One should not be surprised, then, if one finds, as a main inspiration, Jewish thought. We are told that Ernst Bloch would solemnly protest against our interpretation. He did not do so in his lifetime when I sent him my preparatory studies for this chapter. And, moreover, did he not have a deeply Jewish sense of paradox? Did he not himself discover "the counter-Moses within Moses"? He no doubt accepted—and would still accept, were he still alive—our attempt to discover "the counter-Bloch within Bloch."

But, no doubt also, this "counter" does not represent an unshakable opposition, but the counterpoint of a Jewish melody that underlies the life and work of Ernst Bloch from end to end.

THE EXODUS PRINCIPLE

The first strains of that Jewish melody: the social and intellectual milieu in which Ernst Bloch evolved during his earliest creative period, that of *Thomas Münzer*. It was the German-Jewish milieu of about the time of the First World War: Margarete Susman (to whom he dedicated his *Thomas Münzer*), Gustav Landauer, Martin Buber, Franz Rosenzweig, Karl Wolfskehl, Franz Kafka, and Arnold Schönberg, to name only a few of those Jews with whom Ernst Bloch felt a deep affinity—those very ones who were to be sacrificed during the Weimar Republic and then, to the degree that they would still be alive, like Bloch himself, during the Third Reich and the Shoa. The slow but continuous erosion which detached, despite themselves, all these Jews from German society, Bloch perceived in the form of a Jewish biblical legend to which Benjamin Fondane, murdered at Auschwitz, gave its poetic expression and Ernst Bloch its philosophical pattern: the Exodus.

The Exodus principle, taught Ernst Bloch, went back to Moses, who was its inventor of genius. What was the Exodus if not the religious Utopia par excellence, the idea of going forth, of opening up, of passage and arrival? Moses brought Israel out of Egypt. He provided it with the Torah, the seed of all communism (*Ur-Kommunismus:* We should admire the force of this expression which brings Marxism back to Jewish origins of far greater importance than the accident of Karl Marx's Jewish descent). If Moses did not bring Israel into the land of Canaan, at least he was the founder, through the Torah, of the *Heimat,* the Homeland, whose model persists, in defiance of time, changes of epoch, and transient realities, in the appeal of a Utopia whose image may be discerned in the Torah of Moses. This placing of the human Homeland within the sphere of the eternal and the inaccessible made Moses the first, unquestionable creator of Utopia.

The State of Israel in the twentieth century could not, in Bloch's view, as we have said, be the realization of this Utopia, just as the Hebrew state in the biblical period had not been. The Kingdom of Moses does not exist upon the soil of human history. But no more is it in the Heaven of meta-human history which Jesus Christ believed he had created, nor in the cosmos of mega-human history which Karl Marx claimed to have made. It exists in the Promise, that atom whose nucleus is eternity and whose traces are nowhere to be found except only in this model produced by Moses, but which no one had ever seen and which could never be set up.

It is this so typically Jewish principle of non-installation, of non-establishment, of wandering . . . (the Wandering Jew . . . Benjamin Fondane, psalmist of the Exodus at the very period when Ernst Bloch was its scribe—did he not sign some of his poems with the very name of the wandering Jew, Isaac Laquedem?); it is this principle, I say, which led Ernst

Bloch to another principle, even more central to his thought than the Exodus: the principle of *Hope*, the title of the key work of his entire spiritual edifice.

THE PRINCIPLE OF HOPE

I have often protested against Christian attempts to appropriate the Hope of Ernst Bloch. I have to return to this here. No, it is not Christianity "which plays a pivotal role" in Ernst Bloch's philosophy of hope: It is Judaism. A Christian theologian (Paul Schutz) confirms our opinion. In his bulky volume on the *Parousia* (subtitle, "Hope and Prophecy," Heidelberg 1960, 600 pages), he asked the troubling question of "whether Christianity has not remained a debtor of its message of Hope."

It has certainly been a debtor after the Shoa. I need no other proof than Paul Schutz himself. In observing the failure of Christianity, he mentioned Coventry, Dresden, Hiroshima, and the Iron Curtain, but like so many others, he "forgot" the Holocaust and Auschwitz . . .

To be sure, the first reaction of certain Jewish contemporaries of Auschwitz was to conclude the absurdity, the meaninglessness, the impossibility of discovering a significance, human or meta-human, in the event. Like his non-Jewish contemporaries, among whom Jean-Paul Sartre, Camus, and Heidegger are prominent, the Jewish philosopher and Holocaust survivor Theodor Adorno, a friend of Ernst Bloch, found an extreme formula by which to express this despair "after Auschwitz": "After Auschwitz, no poetry, no form of art, no creative affirmation is any longer possible. The interrelationship of things can only be established in a vacant area, in a sort of philosophic no man's land." These lines appeared in the book which Adorno published in Frankfurt in 1967 under the title *Negative Dialectics.*

But, also in Frankfurt, eight years earlier, Ernst Bloch had published *The Principle of Hope,* a monumental work shot through by the electric current of the positive dialectic of Utopia. Why Hope? And what Hope?

I have often drawn attention to the fact that the term Hope is proclaimed in the titles of at least two great books, written by two great Jewish thinkers in the face of Auschwitz: *Nous de l'Espérance* (We the Hopeful) by Edmond Fleg (1949) and *The Principle of Hope* by Ernst Bloch (1959).

One could spend hours pondering the contrast between these two books, which differ in everything: the form, the intention, the style, the basic ideology, the ultimate objective. On the one hand, we have an idyll of the Île de France, a story related by a grandfather to his "unknown grandson," the transposition of a realistic episode through lyrical, impressionist touches, a religious faith strengthened by testing and revolt, a vertically oriented dream whose last images seem to melt away into God. On the other hand, we have two large volumes hewn in the granite of the German language, a proud solitary monologue, a chaotic style borrowing its super-impositions and its discords from dodecaphonic music, a materialist belief strengthened by an excellent knowledge of the Bible, a horizontal utopia whose final words are taken from Karl Marx.

Moreover, what a difference in the experience of the Shoa of each of these two Jewish writers!

Edmond Fleg dwelt at the heart of Job's furnace. He lost his two sons, his only children, in the "Phony War" of 1939, and then he grouped around him the Jewish scouts whom he led, becoming their guide in the Resistance and the *maquis*. The Jewish martyrs of the *maquis* were the spiritual children of Fleg, who emerged from the ordeal like Job, faced with a rising generation of survivors for whom he wrote a *Chant nouveau* (New Song), while being overcome, at the same time, with a terrible sorrow for all those he had lost among the six million destroyed together with his next of kin.

Ernst Bloch, on the other hand, was one of the distant witnesses of the Shoa, since he left Germany very early on and sought refuge in the United States. This distance from events caused more than one Jewish thinker to opt for a pessimistic view. This was not, however, the case with Ernst Bloch, whom an objective observation of the Shoa, seen from without, confirmed in his positive philosophy of Utopia.

The two antithetical books of these two dissimilar men, Edmond Fleg and Ernst Bloch, both turned on the axis of *Hope*, contrary to all expectations. Should we not see in this extreme encounter of these two essentially contradictory spirits the sign of their mutual choice of a Jewish option common to every Jew, the Jewish option of hope? Not just any hope but Jewish hope, gathered in the depths of disaster: the hope of Jeremiah who in the chaotic disintegration of the world saw a Genesis rise up, but a Genesis not at the beginning but at the end—a "dream ahead" in the words of Ernst Bloch, or as Edmond Fleg explained, a continual "return toward the Future." More simply, one might say, a Messianism: The Messianism which Ernst Bloch finds in the Book of Job ("I know that my Messiah liveth") and which Edmond Fleg displays in his last writings, *Vers le monde qui vient* (Towards the World Which Is Coming).

THE JEWISH RESPONSE OF LIBERTY

The source of this wager on Hope bears a name: Liberty, "one of the most frightening ideas to be invented by the harsh and terrible logic of Jewish theology" wrote the novelist Hermann Broch, a contemporary of Edmond Fleg and Ernst Bloch. Philosophical liberty or man's free will, said Hermann Broch, is "something Promethean which no animal possesses: A striving towards an absolute liberty which places him above the natural creation and its laws, although in his physical being he remains subject to them and cannot escape them.'' It was this free will that, in the Middle Ages, Moses Maimonides had recognized as the most dangerous weapon voluntarily placed by God in the hands of men.

It was this "Jewish response of liberty" whose tempestuous hopes were described by Ernst Bloch in his book. He perceived it in the biblical prophets and the Hasidic rabbis. This is what diametrically opposed Moses to Marx, Jeremiah to Cassandra, Bloch's rebellion to that of Prometheus. This is what made the biblical prophets the "pathfinders of history" among whom Ernst Bloch wished to be counted today, and this is what gave Ernst Bloch the courage to break with Moscow at the time of the Hungarian uprising of 1956.

One might, certainly, establish a connection between this Hope and the Christian cardinal virtue, the "little sister" of whom Charles Péguy spoke in accents which moved and affected Bloch with their charm.

But, already in 1919, Franz Rosenzweig had drawn attention to the enormous difference there is between the Christian Hope and Jewish Hope. It was his first lecture in his town of birth, Cassel, which he gave after simultaneously writing, during the war from which he had just emerged, his *Star of Redemption* (which was then being printed) and his correspondence with Eugen Rosenstock which would only be published in 1935, just as this lecture in Cassel entitled ''Spirit and the Periods of Jewish History'' would only be published in 1937. It summarized, in a few pages, the unbridgeable difference which Rosenzweig saw between the Jewish and Christian concepts of the relationship between time and eternity. Christianity possesses the ''already'' of the revelation of Golgotha. This drives it irresistibly towards the kingdom of God. But this same Kingdom of God is possessed by Judaism through the Revelation of Sinai, in a form of eternity requiring a perpetual experience whose main points of demarcation are the Sabbath, the festivals, and the flow of the history whose memory they carry. The role played by the Jew in the Christian dimension is that of a mute servant reminding the Church, each time that its members believe they have tasted God in the bread and the wine, ''Master, remember the ultimate!'' The Jew is a perpetual sign warning the Christian that the end is not yet. He is the man of . . . but here one must quote at length the conclusion of this lecture.

I COMMAND YOU TO HOPE

In it, Rosenzweig recalled a statement of Goethe's, and said that no Greek could have thought of this statement, no Christian, even Goethe, could have conceived it, if the Christians had not, thanks to the Jews, caught the message of the Jewish biblical prophets who here speak through Goethe:

> The Jew does not recognize the demands of time. In the eternity which is special to him, he opposes to time an eternity which time cannot triumph over. By the very fact of his existence, freed as he is from the magic of periods, the Jew preaches silently a word which he brings into the suffering and misery of history, however great their extent, and into the life of peoples, whatever the degree of determinism weighing on them, and into human nature and human culture, whatever their imperfection and uncertainty; a word which we no doubt have the right to render by a celebrated expression of Goethe's, for on Goethe's lips these words have a resonance which they gained entirely from the tongue of the prophets. No Greek ever used in this sense these words which, before the eyes of Time, open the curtain behind which Eternity is hidden. These words are, *"We command you to hope."*

For anyone who is able to judge the true existential value of Ernst Bloch's relationship in 1919 with the group of German-Jewish intellectuals to which Franz Rosenzweig belonged, there can be no further doubt: Rosenzweig's lecture must have circulated among them. It was in contact with him, and not with Péguy, that Bloch must have reacted—he who, at that period, like Rosenzweig himself, was working on his first books: *The Spirit of Utopia* and especially, *Thomas Münzer*. The outcome of *The Principle of Hope* is already present in this early development of Ernst Bloch's thought after the First World War. Certain striking terms which we have brought out in our résumé of Rosenzweig's lecture and our quotation from it are to be found there: "not yet" and "Hope," and—yes, of course—*Jewish hope*, even if it was taken from Goethe, for Goethe, for the Jewish intelligentsia of that period, was classed next to the prophets of the Bible.

Together with "not yet" and "Hope," there was another striking term—the *Sabbath*. It is to be found on the very last page of *Thomas Münzer*, but in the typically Jewish form of the expression (chosen by Ernst Bloch from the spiritual storehouse of Franz Rosenzweig) of which I spoke at the beginning of this excursion into the kingdom of Utopia. I said that it seemed to me to be the jewel in the crown of the sovereign of that kingdom. It was the expression *Die Prinzessin Shabbat*, Princess Sabbath. Of the collection of symbols which Ernst Bloch employed with such dexterity to suggest Utopia, it was the first, the typological Genesis. There is nothing surprising if one finds it also at the end, as the final symbol in *The Principle of Hope*, since "Genesis is not at the beginning but at the end."

PRINCESS SABBATH

The word *Heimat* with which *The Principle of Hope* ends is but a transposition onto a universal plane of the concept *Princess Shabbat* as an emancipated Jew who has lost his way imagines it when he suddenly rediscovers the Jewish roots of his being. On the philosophic level, this undoubtedly represents an encounter of time and eternity as Franz Rosenzweig said, basing himself on Jewish tradition which teaches that "the Sabbath is the mirror of the world to come" (Ernst Bloch would render it "the mirror of Utopia"). On the existential level, however, it is the longing for a lost Homeland: The one which in youth one had some glimpse of, the one which one's backslidings will never allow one to find except in the form of a nostalgia. It was Heinrich Heine who wrote *Die Prinzessin Shabbat* in one of the touching moments of his Return, of his desperate attempt to rediscover a shelter, a home, the family reunited and transfigured by the magic of the Sabbath, one's soul reconciled with oneself and with one's own. We are here in the midst of the emotional experience of the Jewish "meta," and it is this same emotion which underlies the conclusion of Ernst Bloch's *The Principle of Hope*. *Heimat* has been translated by "dwelling place," but that is a wrong rendering. Hitherto, I have rendered *Heimat* by "Homeland," and that is an approximation. A true translation of *Heimat* must stress the indescribable intimacy of this German *Heim* which both soothes and enraptures the straying Jew and brings him both suffering and consolation: the warmth of the Sabbath in his parental home. It is a warmth that has gone forever, except in the dream of regaining it; it is an image of the Inaccessible, a return to oneself which would lead to despair were it not that Utopia had placed on this path of Return the indicative arrow of the *Heim* which promises for tomorrow that which yesterday has passed away, and realizes that promise through the power of Hope.

11

From the Temptation of the Cross to the Star of Redemption: Franz Rosenzweig

A DUEL WITH DEATH

This short life (1886–1929) was divided into two parts which were the stages of a poignant but victorious duel with death.

First of all, there was a victory over spiritual death. This was the first stage, whose turning point was that memorable Yom Kippur of 1913. And, as suddenly as the first act had begun in 1913, the second act appeared in 1922. This time it was a duel with physical death. Franz Rosenzweig was hit by a paralysis which rapidly and progressively deprived him of the use of his muscles, his legs, his arms, and his whole body, even including his power of speech. Only his mind and soul remained lucid. The doctor had predicted one year of lingering death, but owing to the miracle of the joint efforts of Rosenzweig himself, his wife (with whom he communicated through a blinking of the eyes which she was able to interpret and to transpose into words), and his circle, it was the most creative and radiant period of his secluded and suffering-filled existence. Death took him in a few hours on November 10, 1929. He had waged a physical struggle against death and won, for in seven years he had not yielded where others would have given up in seven weeks or seven months. This was the second stage of Franz Rosenzweig's struggle with death. Once again Jewish thought, which had now become one and the same as himself, had been the weapon of his victory.

However, in his thought, the idea of *teshuva* had never, since Yom Kippur 1913, ceased to be active. No one had reflected on this theme or tried to make it the symbol of his Jewish identity as much as he had. Rosenzweig gave basic theoretical definitions of *teshuva* and he put those definitions into practice. He was the very incarnation of Jewish *teshuva*, its philosopher and its model.

139

THE PATIENCE OF REDISCOVERY

In Rosenzweig's *teshuva* there was first of all the coming together of an instant flash of illumination and a long research. Yom Kippur 1913 was his Burning Bush. That day something overwhelming took place, a mystical reversal, concerning which Rosenzweig remained very guarded, but which shone like a beacon in his existence. Then, there was the patient process of rediscovery, the desire to regain lost time, to learn what he did not know and to recreate the Jewish content of his thought and life. To use Rosenzweig's own terminology, he was not content to be the betrothed of *teshuva*, to sense the thunderbolt which had set him ablaze and filled him. He wanted to be the husband of *teshuva* and patiently to raise up the house of Israel with the materials of which he had hitherto been deprived. This is the very meaning which can be given to the Hebrew expression *ba'al teshuva*, which means the "returner." *Ba'al* means master, he who is able to dominate his *teshuva*, but it also means husband, he who is able to travel through life with *teshuva*. Yes, I do mean travel. Here again we have the ambivalence of the Hebrew language. For Maimonides the paths of *teshuva* are ethical principles, rules of conduct, the elements of a code. For Rosenzweig they were truly paths, roads, ways with their dangers of getting lost and the possibility of returning. The *ba'al teshuva* is constantly on the road.

It is on this road that one finds Franz Rosenzweig immediately after Yom Kippur, 1913. This was a road made up of successive discoveries in Judaism, now dazzling, now tentative, from the aleph-bet (alphabet) of the Hebrew language to the creation of a Rosenzweigian thought *sui generis* which at the same time was enshrined in the most authentic Jewish tradition. Even before August 1914, Rosenzweig had discovered the Bible, the Talmud, the Zohar, two contemporary masters (Hermann Cohen and Martin Buber), the Hebrew language, and the Jewish people. Then war broke out. He was conscripted, and on the front, in spare moments, he wrote letters to his converted cousins (and especially to the theologian Eugen Rosenstock who wished to lead him back towards Christianity). These letters enabled Rosenzweig to definitely take his distance towards Christianity, which was perhaps valid for all men, he thought, except for the Jew. For the Jew has no need of the Son in order to enter the Father's dwelling, since he was born within that dwelling and that is where he has to grow and mature.

Rosenzweig's Jewish maturation took place during these same war years. On postcards sent to his mother, he wrote what became his masterpiece, *The Star of Redemption*. This book was published soon after the war, in 1920, at the same time as he submitted his doctoral thesis on Hegel and the State.

He was now at a crossroads of his existence. A university career opened up to him. This promised to be brilliant, but it would have inclined him towards the teaching of *general* philosophy. He deliberately turned his back on it in order to assume the direction of an independent *Jewish* school of higher education in Frankfurt-on-Main, the Lehrhaus. There he created a Jewish center in which the traditional Jewish practices increasingly found a place together with studies and the publication of programmatic writings on Jewish culture, Jewish philosophy, and Jewish politics.

It was there that his illness struck him. His disciples organized the rites of the Sabbath and festivals in his room. Martin Buber came to see him regularly and began with him the translation of the Bible into German. Rosenzweig on his own translated ninety Hebrew poems by Yehuda Halevi and provided them with a commentary. With the help of his wife, and without his terrible illness showing the slightest trace in his thinking, he dictated a correspondence which constituted in itself a sort of encyclopedia of Jewish existence as well as profound studies of the eternal and current problems of Jews and Judaism—assimilation and identity, secularism and religion, diaspora life and Zionism, anti-semitism and the affirmation of Jewish continuity—which appeared in reviews, encyclopedias, and a collection bearing the significant title: *Naharayim, the Country with Two Shores.*

For Franz Rosenzweig's *teshuva* was peculiar in that it extended over two shores. It was simultaneously solid and fragile, elaborated and subject to question, a place of encounter and a path of passage.

No *teshuva* was ever as complete as that of Franz Rosenzweig. It brought back a Jew from the church door to his Jewish identity, the Jewish condition, the Jewish religion. But it never ceased to be a *teshuva:* not an ultimate place of refuge but a dynamic of the way.

ON THE THRESHOLD, IN SEARCH
OF THE KEY

This turning back of the massive evolution of the European Jews in the nineteenth and early twentieth centuries, this reversal of all that the Jews regarded as modern, this return to the sources, was never allowed by Rosenzweig to become a matter of vague romantic formulas. He insisted that it should be a truly existential experience, a revolution of the whole person, a *teshuva*. But was such a *teshuva* possible?

Rosenzweig's contact with the Warsaw Jewish community was enough in itself to make him reply to this question with a clear negative, and arrive at the painful but inescapable conclusion that he would forever remain cut off from that form of Judaism which was the only one to contain the authentic essence of Jewish religious life. A certain effort, however, was needed if one was to see the precious originality of Warsaw's Judaism. Some friends of Rosenzweig's who toured the streets of the Jewish Quarter with him could see nothing at all, but he saw something. He was able to single out those synagogues which were "assimilated, pretentious and cold to the marrow" and the Jews who prided themselves on their elegance and affected to speak Polish. He knew how to distinguish these synagogues and these Jews, so similar to their brothers and sisters in Germany (and who were to be found in Warsaw also), from the warm and simple houses of prayer of the naive and honest Jews who made up the main, the essential part of the Warsaw Jewish community and who held the secret of authentic Jewish life. Rosenzweig, however, also admitted that he had difficulty in seeing, and this was because, in order to understand this secret, one needed a key, and Rosenzweig had utterly missed the opportunity of acquiring that key. The key consisted of an Orthodox education within the family circle from the cradle onwards. A Jew like Rosenzweig whose primary education had taken place in an assimilated environment could at best hope, if he was sufficiently perspicacious, to see authentic Judaism through the window, but the door would never open for him. He was condemned to remain on the threshold.

Where authentic Judaism was concerned, Rosenzweig felt himself to be like a lost child. He knew that his Father's House existed, and in his heart felt a nostalgia for it, but he also felt that he would never be able to regain it. Even when he entered it sometimes, it was as a passing stranger who can be present only as a sad and curious observer of a spectacle in which his own proper role as an actor is condemned to remain unfilled. He had a marvelous knowledge of the décor of that House, of the language which was spoken there, the customs which were practiced, but in much the same way as one might be acquainted with some exotic and permanently inaccessible region. Rosenzweig remained outside in exile, with an intense consciousness of this Kingdom whose gates of intimate access were closed against him.

REDISCOVERING THE LANGUAGE

In Rosenzweig's case, the sentiment of exile was sharpened by a somewhat unexpected factor: that of language. For this practiced linguist, this master of the German language who was to devote long years to the fruitful task of translating the Bible and Yehuda Halevi, words had an exceptional intellectual and emotional value. No less than ideas, they are indicative of essence. Now, Rosenzweig felt, and felt increasingly every day, that he was cut off from the language which contained and expressed the Jewish essence. By means of working wonders, he succeeded in extracting from the German language shades of meaning which could render the biblical magic. Through the force of perseverance, he acquired a well-based and superior knowledge of classical Hebrew. But if, by its very nature, German could not claim to be an authentic expression of Judaism, Hebrew could not claim that either. The Jewish soul—that of the European ghetto, at any rate—had forged itself a language of its own. Intermediate between Hebrew and German, grounded in Yiddish without being the same, and integrated with cantilations, modulations, and essential rhythms, the language of the study of Talmud in the schools of Eastern Europe sprang up from the intimate depths of the Jewish soul. For the authentic Jew, this idiom exemplified the harmony between life and language, between experience and the expression of it. It was an inseparable part of him, and it helped to reinforce the organic unity of his personality. But, for a fragmented Jew like Rosenzweig, this language retained an exotic character. It was beyond his reach although it tempted him like a mirage.

Throughout his new life of Jewish studies, over and above the anxiety which assailed him sometimes when faced with the slowness of his progress in mastering the Talmud and the vastness of the intellectual realm which he still had to unravel, Rosenzweig was haunted with another worry, which gradually began to appear like an unquestionable certitude: He lacked the linguistic instrument—the truly Jewish language, which the Warsaw schoolboy imbibed with the air of the ghetto—which would allow him an intuitive penetration of Talmudic knowledge and would give him the comforting impression of not drifting without a compass on an uncharted ocean but of sensing, beyond distant horizons, the presence of ever-familiar coasts. He was only able to use fragments, isolated expressions of this language, which he did in confidential moments when communicating with people who were connected with him by a spiritual closeness and who understood his merest hint. Thus, his favorite pupil was not a disciple but a *boher:* He himself had no ambition of becoming a rabbi, but said he would like to possess the qualities of a *rav:* The biblical commentators were called *meforshim* and the textual divergence between the first and second chapter of Genesis was described as a *plugto*. With these words, Rosenzweig entered for a few moments into the kingdom of Jewish study, but these were only ephemeral probings. The illusion quickly passed, and it was with a redoubled disappointment that Rosenzweig found that, in order to express his Jewish thought in German, he was left with his rabbis, his Bible critics, and his sources J and E.

One word alone escaped this evil spell: *lernen*. It so chanced that this word signified ''study'' at one and the same time in German and in the Jewish language. In saying *lernen*, Rosenzweig had thus the inestimable privilege of expressing himself as both a Western and an Eastern Jew. In one breath, he could make himself understood by either; in one breath, he could refer to Western university education and sacred Talmudic studies and uphold—for himself and others—the illusion that, since both are covered by the same term, the two forms of study are—or at least can be—identical. It was, in fact, one of Rosenzweig's spiritual successes to have plumbed both types of study in a single dimension. Here, aided by the secret of a word which simultaneously applied to both, Rosenzweig succeeded in achieving a precious synthesis. The same, however, was not true in the realm of action, where the German terms *tun, Gesetz,* and *Gebot* had nothing in common with the corresponding Jewish terms of *mekayem, Torah,* and *mitzvah.* It was in vain in that Rosenzweig multiplied attempts to create a suitable German term. Nothing availed. Here, the secret of the Jewish language remained intractable. The linguistic dichotomy here was a sort of visible sign of the tear whereby Rosenzweig was convinced that he was definitively separated from authentic Jewish activity. But, in the invisible sphere, is anything really definitive for the *ba'al teshuva?*

THE "PERSONALISM" OF TESHUVA: THE RETURN TO OBSERVANCE

If Rosenzweig was happy with the role of *ba'al teshuva,* if he saw it as a dominant feature of his Jewish destiny, that was in great part because it corresponded with his fundamental philosophical leanings. Rosenzweig's "personalism" found in the idea of the *ba'al teshuva* an almost natural opportunity to express itself in Jewish terms and concepts. It had a tendency towards definitions which were perhaps no longer Jewish from the point of view of classical theology, but which an existential theology could justifiably consider traditional and valid. Thus, Rosenzweig treated as an end that which classical theology regarded only as a means. The aim assigned by dogmatism to the path of the *ba'al teshuva,* which is to become a wholly observant Jew, is set back by Rosenzweig in the course of that very path, which thus passes, with regard to the scale of values, from the relative to the absolute. The "returner" is not a man whose function is to find or to rediscover the Home which he had lost or which he had never known. Returning is his law, and it is precisely in his path, in his quest, in his search perpetually set in doubt, perpetually subject to wanderings, eternally promised for a future which never comes, that the absolute significance of his destiny is hidden.

Rosenzweig brought into the concept of the *ba'al teshuva* the dominant themes of a personalism which, in its forms of expression if not in its contents, is quite close to that of Pascal. Certain formulas used by Rosenzweig throughout his correspondence belong to a terminology common to all personalists. "Not to do violence to oneself, not to precede oneself: To use only one's legs to walk with, not a stick, and above all, no crutches." Others are clearly inspired by mystical thought. "To await, even though with regret, even though with the sentiment of never finding them—to await the biographical hours of grace."

But what theological significance can "waiting for grace" have in Judaism, when the observance of the Law in Judaism is not submitted to the criterion of grace but to that of effort? Seeing that the Law is mandatory, observance required, and the practical ordinances for the observance of the Law spelled out in accepted codes, is not the Jew who claims to wait for grace in order to submit himself to the yoke of the Law simply looking for a loophole, is he not really tearing himself away from the Kingdom of the Law, and is he not concealing by the word "grace," which is meaningless in a theology of law, the fact that, despite his affirmations, he is not expecting anything? Jewish theology, like Christian theology, demands an adhesion on the part of the believer to the principles of the community, whether the community is the synagogue or the church. It is enough for the Christian believer to claim sincerely that he is awaiting Grace for him to be in a communion of waiting with his brethren, but the Jewish believer can only show his communion with the Jewish people by observance, and the criterion of this observance is not left to the individual: it is established by the community. Although the criterion varies from one period to another, it is nevertheless, at any given period, the application of such and such a body of observances that defines the Law, and anyone who, for subjective reasons, rejects all or part of that body, places himself outside the Law.

Rosenzweig had an experience of this in relation to the observance of the Sabbath, as he explained in a letter to the liberal rabbi Benno Jacob. In the first years of his *teshuva*, he had applied the prohibition against writing on the Sabbath only to purely professional correspondence, but he continued writing to his family and friends. He had thus applied to the Sabbath the criteria of "pleasant" and "irksome" not recognized by the traditional Jewish Law, but which liberal Judaism extended to the Sabbath rest as a whole. This went on until, one Sabbath, one of his close collaborators, speaking to him about problems related to the Lehrhaus, asked him to write out some notes since, in any case, he wrote on the Sabbath. "It was only this experience, which proved to me the impossibility of having shades of difference if everyone did not carry them out in the same way, that then brought me heavy-heartedly to an Orthodox practice in this particular domain." "Heavy-heartedly, in this particular domain": These words show that, defeated on this point by experience, he nevertheless refused to make it into a general rule. If, in the observance of the Sabbath, he had attained a limited "Orthodox" objective, he nevertheless remained distant from innumerable similar objectives in numerous domains, and, placing reflection above the accidents of daily experience, he affirmed that, in its essence, this distance was an unquestionable virtue for the *ba'al teshuva*.

Taking an extreme situation, Rosenzweig even declared himself willing to run the risk of being cut off from the historic community. "People like us," he wrote to his pupil Rudolf Hallo, "cannot purely and simply return to the arms of the synagogue. Ours is always a situation apart. We need the ancient historical community, and at the same time we can never simply identify ourselves with it.''

RETURNING TO THE ABSOLUTE

But Rosenzweig did not receive his conviction of being in exile only from his personal fate as a Western, emancipated Jew which imprisoned him in an irreversible historical process. If he was cut off from the true Kingdom, this was because, in the final analysis, every man, whoever he may be, is condemned to wander around the Essence without ever being able to attain it and to catch sight of the Absolute without ever being able to comprehend it. This is the very definition which the Bible gives of the human situation before God. How could a man like Rosenzweig, nurtured on the Bible, accepting, for his part, an existential solidarity with the biblical message, escape such a destiny?

Rosenzweig knew that this was not a comfortable situation, but what could he do about it? The idea had not been present in his thought from the beginning, and the forms of revelation had been analyzed in *The Star of Redemption* in 1918 with too much optimism, had been too steeped in classical notions for such a contorted idea of things to find its place there. In the last pages, however, when the analysis of revelation was taken up again in the light of Jewish mysticism, the triangular edifice linking up God, the world, and man is seen to be able to hold together only if there is a rethinking of the Absolute, adventurous and full of risks. It was in the course of the vicissitudes of his biblical researches that Rosenzweig suddenly realized the fragility of the theories of the much-respected biblical criticism. The contradictions within God, man's re-enactions of similar situations, defined by exegesis as literary duplications from different historical levels, now suddenly appeared to Rosenzweig as basic differences by means of which the Bible illuminated for a brief but fulgurating instant the incertitudes of the radical relationship between man and God.

Rosenzweig's intuitions were finally confirmed by a reading of Kafka. It happened too late for a broad spiritual confrontation to take place between the two thinkers who were interconnected by so many subterranean channels. When Rosenzweig read *The Castle* in May 1927, Kafka had been dead for three years, and the ailing Rosenzweig had only two more years to live. But, as we have already recalled, he noted in a letter: ''The people who wrote the Bible apparently imagined God in the same way as Kafka does. I have never yet read a book which reminded me as much of the Bible as his novel *The Castle*. Moreover, reading it is no amusement . . . ''

One can well imagine that Rosenzweig might have interpreted his sickness in the light of Kafka's universe and that he applied certain ideas of

The Metamorphosis and *The Penal Colony* to himself, but that was not the case. Apart from the fact that Rosenzweig always spoke of his illness with a remarkable reserve, he never agreed to consider his state of sickness as "abnormal." The intellectual and spiritual world he built around himself corresponded to the needs of a physically normal person, and he was content to live in it as though he were well, reacting to the consequences of his illness as regrettable but unimportant accidents. He discovered man's abnormality, and consequently his own, beyond sickness and health, in the relations, at once necessary and impossible, between man and God. Thus, the world of Kafka's *Castle* corresponded admirably to that of Rosenzweig, and by his themes and images he intensified Rosenzweig's awareness of his exile. Like Kafka, Rosenzweig felt himself to be living in the outskirts of the Absolute: He had a splendid view of the City of God, of the Kingdom where divine service was performed with integrity and spontaneity. He corresponded with the inhabitants of the Kingdom and received their messages. But, again like Kafka, he found that these mysterious and contradictory messages greatly confused his situation, and depriving him of the key for reaching the interior of the Kingdom, made him a perpetually lost member of the Elect, an Adam doomed to perpetual exile.

The parallel between Rosenzweig and Kafka, however, has very precise limits. Between the two, there was the difference that exists between incident and drama, between anxiety and tragedy.

Earlier, I showed how the sense of having been born too late disoriented Kafka's will in an irremediable manner. Rosenzweig's willpower, on the other hand, remained intact; only his capacities were limited. Rosenzweig's return to Judaism was wholehearted, even—and especially—in those things which he was unable to accomplish. While progressing, in the practical upbuilding of his life, towards an entirely traditional orthodoxy, he never agreed to be labeled as Orthodox so as to leave the field open to an unlimited investigation of the possible, allowing for a residue.

This residue can and ought to appear to the observer (as it did to Rosenzweig himself) as a perpetual deficiency. But what was lacking in Rosenzweig's Judaism as a whole was as indispensable to a fullness as the interstices in a stained-glass window or the silences in a symphony. The inaccessible was appropriated by him and embedded in his will to Judaism. These were "holes" which he was unable to fill, but he measured and delimited the lines and hollows with a lucidity which gave the Jewish harmony of his personality a touch of added splendor.

12

From Baptism to Kol Nidre—
Arnold Schönberg

In the same way as his work, Arnold Schönberg's personality was controversial, mysterious, contradictory, disputed. The revolution he effected in art finally gained acceptance even in his lifetime, but some of his major works—the opera *Moses and Aaron, Jacob's Ladder, The Biblical Path, Modern Psalms*—remained incomplete, and their fragments were presented to the public only after Schönberg's death in some cases, while others are still waiting for a première which will perhaps never take place.

Such also was Schönberg's thought—unfinished, fragmented, hinted at in a series of paradoxes in which the interpreter loses himself in conjectures which are in danger of betraying him: "O Word, Word which I am lacking!" This cry which Schönberg gives to Moses is valid for Schönberg himself. It is also valid for the place which Judaism occupies in Schönberg's thought. It is valid also for the place within that thought occupied by *teshuva*.

THE WRITTEN DOCUMENT OF A TESHUVA

What? Did I not refer at the beginning of this book to the document of July 24, 1933? Did not this document, signed by a rabbi, by Marc Chagall, and by Schönberg himself, signify that Schönberg returned to the Jewish community? In that case, he must once have left it. On July 24, 1933, in the synagogue of rue Copernic in Paris, he returned to it. What more striking act of *teshuva* could be imagined? Is this document not sufficient in order for Arnold Schönberg to be described as a *ba'al teshuva*? Is that not perfectly obvious?

No, it is not obvious to everyone. The significance, the importance, and even the authenticity of the document of July 24, 1933, have been disputed. Some biographers simply fail to mention it: They deliberately ob-

149

scure the salient features of Schönberg's Judaism, and sometimes his Judaism as such. Worse still, one reference to Jesus—a single one—in the *Prayers* composed towards the end of his life, and a reference to the Gospels in a work of his youth, have been sufficient for them to claim that Schönberg's religiosity was of Christian inspiration. Did not this Jew-by-birth convert to Protestantism at the age of twenty-four, in 1898 (an act which was duly registered and which is considered, in this case, as irrefutable)? There never was a return to Judaism, it is claimed. The Jewish themes in Schönberg's work were for him what the Old Testament is for the Christian in relation to the New: A relic which is precious but superseded (Willy Reich).

Paradoxically, the authenticity of this document has been questioned by the proponents of a thesis diametrically opposite to the preceding one: the thesis of a Jewish continuity in Schönberg's life and work. Jesus? The Gospel according to Luke? These, it is claimed, were elements of a general culture of which Christianity formed part without having any special position. Who would dare to claim that Edmond Fleg or Martin Buber or Marc Chagall were not Jewish or became Christians, simply because in their work they provided—far more than their contemporary Arnold Schönberg—a place for Jesus and the saints of the Church? The conversion of Schönberg to Protestantism? An act of purely social significance, an entryticket to bourgeois society, at a time when Schönberg was about to marry Mathilde, the sister of his teacher and patron, the conductor Alexander von Zemlinski. But where his heart, his convictions, his religious feelings were concerned, it is claimed that Schönberg remained Jewish. "In his work," wrote Jan Meyerovits,

> Christianity played no role. The Jewish side of his creations is of exclusively Jewish inspiration, unlike many Jewish composers, for instance Meyerbeer, Halévy, and Milhaud, who remained true to their faith but whose works contain many Christological features. In 1933 it became publicly known that in Paris Schönberg had returned to Judaism. He himself continually vigorously denied this story and repeated on various occasions that his work proved that he had long before returned to Judaism. The ceremony of return in Paris which is so often mentioned seems to have been entirely invented by a certain Dr. Marianoff, eager for publicity.

In fact, the document undoubtedly does exist: Its authenticity is undeniable. The original is preserved in the Arnold Schönberg Archives in Los Angeles. Professor Hans Stuckenschmidt, one of Schönberg's pupils, gave a photographic reproduction of it on page 335 of his great book, *Schönberg,* published in Zurich in 1974. One of the two witnesses, Marc Chagall, was universally known. He could not have been suspected of complicity in a false testimony through an "eagerness for publicity." As for Rabbi Louis-Germain Lévy, he was a man of absolute integrity. He would certainly have protested against a forgery, but he never cast doubt on the authenticity of the document.

And Schönberg himself? His "vigorous denials"? His "assertion repeated on various occasions that he had long before returned to Judaism"?

We have two irrefutable written proofs from Schönberg of the genuineness of the act and consequently of the authenticity of the document. The first was the private diary in which Schönberg noted, in a stenographic style, the main points of his life. The date July 23, 1933, is marked by the work *Rückkehr*, which cannot mean anything else than the ceremony of *teshuva* in the rue Copernic. A second proof was a letter to his pupil Alban Berg on August 8, 1933, in which Schönberg regretted the publicity with which Dr. Marianoff, through his awkward handling, had surrounded the ceremony. This shows that the ceremony did take place. We shall soon realize that Schönberg's reservations with regard to Dr. Marianoff were in no way due to the fact that he considered his official return to Judaism as something banal which was not worth speaking about in public. On the contrary, it was the importance of this act which made Schönberg hope that an awkward publicity would not depreciate or turn against himself and the Jewish community an act of *teshuva* which he regarded as serious and above all as necessary.

It was necessary for the outside world: The world had to know that Arnold Schönberg was no longer a Christian, that he had returned to Judaism. But it was also necessary for Schönberg's internal development, for there existed within him, in his life and in his work, an adventure, a drama of *teshuva*.

CONVERSATIONS WITH
(AND ABOUT) GOD

The revolution which Schönberg brought about in modern art began in 1912. It was then that he composed and successfully had performed a musical accompaniment to the poem *Verklärte Nacht* by the famous socialist visionary Richard Dehmel, but this success was short-lived and did not put an end to the miserable bohemian existence which Schönberg had led since his birth in Vienna in 1874. He had already reached full maturity—he was thirty-two years old. The burden of a difficult youth still weighed on him. Having lost his father at the age of fifteen and having left school without a diploma and without a profession, he retained a deep gratitude to three men who recognized his musical vocation: Gustav Mahler, Alexander von Zemlinski, and Walter Pieau. The first was one of the masters of post-Wagnerian music. He was Jewish by birth but converted to Christianity in 1897 and remained a Christian. The second, a Christian-born conductor of the same age as Schönberg, gave his friend his musical education and offered him the hand of his sister Mathilde, on one condition, however: baptism, made more acceptable by the prestigious example of Gustav Mahler and also by the friendship of Walter Pieau, an opera singer and a believing Protestant. Schönberg's conversion to Protestantism on March 25, 1898, must be seen in this sociological context. In any case, it did not find any particular confirmation in Schönberg's soul. When confronted with the question, "What are you?," his reply was vague, groping: "I am atheist, unbelieving, freethinking"—"as my father was," he added.

But a formula he used in a letter of that period touched his real religious identity: "My position is dialectical."

Schönberg's parents were a dialectical couple. His father had been a freethinker, but he was no longer alive. His mother, revered by her son, was a believing, pious, practising Jewess. A brother of his mother was a talented musician and a minister-officiant in a Vienna synagogue. He remained faithfully attached to his nephew Arnold after and despite his conversion.

It was his mother's influence which won the day. The dialectic came into the open in 1912, at the very moment when Schönberg, after years of apprenticeship, felt that he too was becoming a Master.

In his correspondence with Richard Dehmel, one would expect him to evoke the problems of particular interest to the poet whose musical interpreter Schönberg was: socialism, aesthetics, art-for-art's sake or "committed" art. However, the thing which tormented Schönberg and which he unburdened himself to Dehmel about was, paradoxically, the problem of prayer and particularly the significance of prayer for modern man.

Schönberg was literally tormented by this problem which was never more to leave him. It was his argument with God whose echoes were to combine, dissolve, and re-combine in words and sounds, the argument of a Jewish *ba'al teshuva*. It was to continue until the final chords of *Modern Psalms*, written a few weeks before his death and left unfinished. When Schönberg spoke about them, he called them "Psalms, Prayers, and other Conversations with (and about) God." The first sketches for it already appeared in a strange work in which he was engaged in the midst of the First World War—in a period when, according to his civil status, Schönberg was a Christian.

This work, which accompanied him for the rest of his life, was called *Jacob's Ladder.*

JACOB'S LADDER

Schönberg did not decide on this title immediately. First he thought of *Jacob's Struggle* (his struggle with the angel, Genesis 32). If he finally chose the ladder (Genesis 28) rather than the struggle, it was in order to stress the connection between his musical revolution and his Jewish religious feelings, but there was nevertheless a struggle, even if it was only between the words and the sounds. There was also a Jewish struggle between the sphere of action (the Ten Commandments) and the sphere of passivity (Hear, O Israel!)

On this biblical theme, Schönberg developed a whole cosmic, universal pacifistic theology, but the music did not follow the words. Only a few isolated, tentative, awkward fragments date from that period. Only thirty years later, in 1947, after the Second World War, did Schönberg, now an "official" Jew after his "reconversion" of 1933, return to the *Ladder*. He made no change in the text, so prophetic was it, and no more than in 1917 did he succeed in finding the musical language which fitted it.

This unfinished work (which was performed for the first time in 1961, ten years after Schönberg's death, in his native city of Vienna) was under consideration throughout his life and thus demonstrates the persistence of his religious temperament but also his conscious or unconscious inability to express it in universal terms. It was only in specifically Jewish religious terms that Schönberg could be fully and supremely creative and, above all, innovative.

The general structure of Schönberg's revolution in the history of modern music already had some Jewish associations. It has been pointed out that the dodecaphonic system is based on the number twelve: the number of the tribes of Israel or the sons of Jacob. I will add that this system is based on a dislocation of the classic scale: in German *Ton-Leiter* or ladder of sounds, in Hebrew, *sulam,* ladder. We have just pointed out Schönberg's essential inability to transpose the biblical theme of *Jacob's Ladder* into musical terms. This was not merely a matter of adapting the words. The text of the libretto is so concentrated, shot through with the mystical struggle of the individual with eternity, that it is impossible not to see the solution, the redemption (*Auf-lösung, geula* in Hebrew) in dissonance, characteristic of the clash of irreconcilables. This is the theology of the Zohar, of the Maharal of Prague, of Hasidism, in which Schönberg found the key to the ladder linking the human and the divine, but this ladder cannot be projected in the classical scale. Salvation cannot come from the scale (*Leiter*), but from Jacob's ladder (*Jakobs-Leiter*).

Also the allusion at a certain moment in the first sketch of *Jacob's Ladder* to the Gospel according to Luke ought not to mislead us. This is not a reference to Christianity but to a Jew in the New Testament who told Jesus: "I have observed all these things from my youth upwards . . . " (Luke 18:21). "All these things" were the commandments, the summary of the Jewish Law made by Jesus in verse 20. "From my youth upwards . . . ": isn't this Schönberg himself speaking, remembering his mother who observed the Jewish Law in simple sincerity?

VICISSITUDES OF TESHUVA—THE "META"
AND THE "ANTI"

As I said, it was the year 1917. It was a first apex of the return to Judaism. The death of Mathilde and marriage to Gertrude Kolish, a Jewess (the sister of the founder of the celebrated Kolish quartet) enabled Schönberg to conceive of an "official" return to Judaism which he was to carry out publicly in the year 1933, when Germany was veering towards the forces of demonism, but the ceremony in rue Copernic on July 24, 1933, (at which Gertrude was present together with Dr. Marianoff and Marc Chagall) boomeranged against Schönberg. The Viennese press took hold of it and used it to wage a fierce anti-semitic campaign. The Jew Schönberg, they said, already stateless, has now become a traitor to his religion. Doubly a Judas, he sells Germany and sells Christianity for—there can be no doubt about it—the money of the Rothschilds!

How well one can understand Schönberg's regrets at the awkward publicity given by Dr. Marianoff (in *Paris-Soir*) to the ceremony in rue Copernic, but it is also clear that Schönberg desired that ceremony with all his heart. Only, he was caught in the predicament described by Jakob Wassermann in his text "In Vain." Whatever the Jew does, he is branded as Judas. If he converts to Christianity, he is a traitor to the Jews. If he returns to Judaism, he is a traitor to the Christians. If he hides his conversions, he is a coward. If he declares them, he is asked who is paying.

Yet Schönberg remained steadfast even in such a situation. Where others yielded, he took up the challenge and entered the fray.

Already in 1923, the very year in which Jakob Wassermann described the impasse in which the "anti" had placed the Jew of German culture, and ten years before the rise to power of Hitler, Schönberg also described that same impasse ten years before his official return to Judaism. In two violent letters, he hurled a "j'accuse" against his friend, the (non-Jewish) painter Kandinsky, and, through him, against the demonic masks of the "anti." Kandinsky sympathized with the Brownshirts of Hitler's putsch in the Munich beer cellar. He favored the exclusion of the Jews from German society, but he declared himself ready to make an "exception" for his friend Schönberg whom he admired and respected, even if he did have "the Jews' crooked nose."

Schönberg's response was more than biting. Like Wassermann's analysis, it cut right to the very heart of the Gordian knot of the "anti":

> . . . What I have been compelled to learn this last year, I have now finally understood and shall never forget: I am neither a German, nor a European, nor even a man (the vilest of Europeans throws his race in my face). I am a Jew.

I am quite content! Today I hope for no exception with regard to myself; I do not object to being tarred with the same brush as the others. For I have seen that the other side (which is no longer in any way exemplary for me) are also all to be tarred with the same brush. Someone whom I had thought to be on the same level as myself I have seen associating himself with this band. I have heard that even Kandinsky only saw those actions of the Jews which were despicable and only those despicable actions which were committed by the Jews, and consequently I lose any hope of reaching an understanding. It was a dream. There are two humanities—definitely! . . .

. . . When I am walking in the street and someone scrutinizes me in order to find out whether I am Jewish or Christian, I can hardly tell him that I am precisely the one for whom Kandinsky makes an exception, although in any case their Hitler is not of this opinion. And that is why this kind thought could not be of any use to me even if it were inscribed on my bosom like the placards carried by blind beggars in such a way that everyone can read them. Could not Kandinsky foresee all that, could he not sense what was going to happen? . . .

Every Jew shows by his crooked nose not only his own guilt, but that of all the crooked noses that are absent . . .

How can Kandinsky tolerate that I should be injured? How can he support a policy which makes possible my exclusion from my natural field of activity? How can he refrain from fighting a conception of the world which prepares new St. Bartholemew's nights, where the darkness will be such that one will not be able to read on my breast that I am an exception to be spared? . . .

. . . I must conclude. . . . I realize now that I have made a very great moral and tactical mistake. I have accepted the discussion, I have entered into a polemic, I have defended myself. In doing so, I have forgotten that it is a matter neither of law nor of absence of law, nor of truth, nor of falsehood, nor of knowledge, nor of ignorance, but of power relationships. . . . I forgot that the discussion had no sense since in any case I shall not be heard, that there is no wish to understand, if it is not that of not hearing what the other says . . .

The Trial and *The Castle* of Kafka!

It was a situation which Schönberg soon experienced after having sensed it as a theoretical threat, for, two years after this polemic with Kandinsky, an "exceptional" status was officially offered to Arnold Schönberg. He was chosen, in an unexpected and gratifying manner, to succeed Busoni as Professor of Composition at the Prussian Academy of Arts in Berlin in 1925. This nomination put an end to half a century of a nomadic and materially difficult existence. "Nomination for life, irrevocable," said the decree signed by the president of the Academy, Max von Schillings, on September 17, 1925. The Jew-Christian Schönberg now appeared to be protected from any intrusion of the "anti." Illusion! As Schönberg had foreseen, the irrevocable is irrevocable for everyone except the Jew. In 1933, Schönberg was deprived of his post as a result of the application of the Jewish Statute. The order of September 18, 1933, revoking the irrevocable, was signed by this same president Max von Schillings!

The greatness of Schönberg was to have remained true to himself, to his Jewish faith, to belief in the Jewish vocation.

The letter to Kandinsky revealed a cast of mind which, in this same year 1923, Wassermann or Kafka did not possess. After pointing out the impossible situation of the Jew, they allowed themselves to pass from discouragement to despair, ending with absurdity. Schönberg, on the other hand, sensed the "meta" within the "anti." The provocation was for him a recall to vocation: "What will anti-semitism lead to if it is not to violence?," he asked in his letter to Kandinsky, "Is it so difficult to imagine? Will they be content to deprive the Jews of their rights? Einstein, Mahler, myself, and many others will be suppressed.

But one thing is certain: they will not be able to exterminate the most vigorous elements of Judaism's capacity of resistance, thanks to which it has been able to survive without protection in the face of the rest of humanity. They are apparently so strong that they are always able to fulfill the mission God has given them: To survive in exile without admixture nor renunciation until the hour of deliverance! . . .

SURVIVING IN EXILE UNTIL THE
HOUR OF DELIVERANCE

Polemics was not Schönberg's only weapon. In the ten years 1923 to 1933, between his break with Kandinsky and his dismissal by the Nazis, he worked enthusiastically on two Jewish dramatic works: *The Biblical Path* and *Moses and Aaron.*

The Biblical Path consisted of a libretto which its author, Schönberg himself, did not succeed in transposing into musical terms (a repetition of the creative phenomenon of *Jacob's Ladder*). The hero of the piece, Max Aruns, combined in himself the idea of Moses and Aaron. He was torn apart by the conflict between the ideal and the real. He was searching, on behalf of the Jewish people, for a land where he could freely set up the City of God. One can detect here, implicitly, the "territorialist" doctrine: Seeing that Palestine is ruled out by the Turks or the British, why not look for some country other than Palestine? Herzl thought of it at the time of the Uganda project, and Zangwill remained a "territorialist" until the Balfour Declaration. Itshak Steinberg was one of the last adherents of territorialism, even after the creation of the State of Israel. For Arnold Schönberg, territorialism was merely a hypothesis, formulated only in order to be rejected at once. Max Aruns failed, and died. The true solution could only be the Zionism of Zion.

Moses and Aaron, although brought together in the imaginary character of Max Aruns, appear separate in Schönberg's opera as they are in the Bible. The opera consisted of three acts, of which he wrote the full libretto, but he only found the music which corresponded to the first two.

The philosophical theme of compromise versus the Absolute revealed a new aspect in this opera: that of *teshuva*, connected with Yom Kippur.

Yom Kippur did not come into being in the desert as an established "normal" ritual institution. It grew out of a drama: The tragedy of the Golden Calf, in which Aaron had accepted a compromise and even a sort of "conversion" to the idol, while Moses had embodied the Absolute, breaking the Tablets of the Law, soiled by the orgy which had so closely followed the sublime Revelation of the Decalogue on Sinai. Idolatry, inner moral rupture in the case of Aaron, the metaphysical rupture expressed externally by the act of Moses—could all this be repaired by a return, a *teshuva?* Yes. The worst of aberrations can find its redemption through the institution of the twenty-four hours of Yom Kippur. One cannot descend any lower, mark the distance between God and man to a greater extent than through the Golden Calf. One will not be able to ascend higher, build a bridge between God and man more effectively than through the fasting, prayer, and silence of Yom Kippur.

Thus, the theme of prayer, which had haunted Schönberg for so many years, was directly connected to that of *teshuva*. It is permissible to suppose that the years 1930–1932 in which Schönberg worked intensely on his opera prepared the way for his solemn act of *teshuva* in rue Copernic in 1933. The shock of the encounter with the "anti" in the fatal year of the coming of the Third Reich certainly played a part, but the element of the "meta," gradually brought to fruition in the score and libretto of *Moses and Aaron*, also exercised its impact. Yom Kippur was not absent from the ceremony of July 24, 1933, in Paris.

I should like to point to a coincidence which provides food for thought for anyone who is aware of the extent to which Schönberg looked for signs and meanings in numbers, dates, and the arithmetic of existence. The opera *Moses and Aaron* was never performed in Schönberg's lifetime. The first performances took place in Hamburg in 1964. As for Paris, the city in which Schönberg returned to the Jewish community in 1933 in the attitude of a *ba'al teshuva* on Yom Kippur, it so happened that its third performance, at the Paris Opera, coincided with the evening of October 6, 1973. The Jews of Paris had just learned that at two o'clock in the afternoon on that October 6, the Egyptian and Syrian armies had launched the Yom Kippur War against Israel. . . .

A MILITANT EXILE—A ZIONIST POLITICAL DOCTRINE

His dismissal did not surprise Schönberg. He went ahead and left Germany for France.

He could have gone to his native Vienna or to Prague, where he had pressing invitations for concerts, for seminars, for musical study groups. If he decided to go to France, it was because he wished to share the fate of the Jewish émigrés who were then flocking to the land of liberty. His was a militant exile, devoted to the service of his Jewish brethren whom he tried to help to the best of his ability.

In the archives which George Alter, the longstanding impresario and admirer of Schönberg, bequeathed to the National Library in Jerusalem in 1975, I found the following hitherto unpublished letter to Alter from Rudolf Kolish: "Don't count on Schönberg for a recital in Prague. He no longer has a fixed address: now in Paris, now in Arcachon, now in Geneva. . . . What he does have is an *idée fixe:* to help his Jewish brethren in distress, to help get them out of the German inferno. He no longer writes a note of music and has put himself entirely at the disposal of the World Jewish Congress which is being set up to prevent the worst . . . "

The list of articles, reflections, and drafts found in Schönberg's archives dating from the year 1933 is long and eloquent. It amounts to a real collection of Jewish writings, and these are dominated by two main ideas, which are that there is a need for a radically new Jewish policy, and that it must lead to the creation of a single, united Jewish political party. Some of the titles of these pages, all dating from 1933, are:

The Jewish Question.
Notes on Jewish Politics.
Studies on the Jewish Problem.
A New Realistic Jewish Policy.
A Program of Aid and Reconstruction for a United Jewish Party.
The Jewish Government in Exile.
The Four-point Program.

A four-point program, a government in exile. . . . Schönberg felt himself to be the spokesman for this government which did not yet exist.

He did not forget the call of Zionism and launched an appeal to all the exiled musicians for the creation of a symphony orchestra in Palestine. The idea was received with enthusiasm by many musicians, but it remained only an idea. It was carried out only in 1937, by Bronislav Hubermann. To direct the first concert in Tel Aviv, he brought over Arturo Toscanini from the United States.

Schönberg was also in the States from October 1933 onwards. Exhausted by his feverish activity and without material resources, he accepted the position of Professor of Composition at the Boston Conservatoire. To his great surprise, he was acclaimed as a master in America, and from 1934 onwards he found excellent working conditions in Los Angeles.

On the liner *Île de France,* which took him to America, he had but one regret: not that of leaving Europe, but of not having headed for Palestine. The sense of exile grew sharper: Schönberg was thwarted of the fruits of his Zionist dream. From this he derived a psychological compensation: an even closer identification with the fate of his people through the medium of his art.

THE PRESENCE OF EVENTS: THE SHOA
AND THE STATE OF ISRAEL

Far from estranging him, America, on the contrary, drew him closer to the two contradictory phases of Jewish history which took place in Europe and Asia, and which Schönberg witnessed: the *Shoa* and the creation of the State of Israel. His creativity in the immediate postwar years proves it.

A Warsaw Survivor (1947) is hewn out of the living flesh of the suffering and heroism of the martyred Jewish people. In his opus 46, Schönberg recorded the testimony of a survivor of the Warsaw Ghetto, using words and adding only two elements: rapid, emotive sounds and in conclusion, the "old forgotten prayer," the Shema Israel. What others hewed in stone in Warsaw and Jerusalem, Schönberg expressed in the dimension of sound.

On the basis of six stanzas by Dagobert Runes, Arnold Schönberg composed his Ode to Joy on the Restoration of the State of Israel: *Dreimal tausend Jahre* (Three Times a Thousand Years).

Moses was not able to enter the Promised Land but his people entered it. And here is the miracle: After three times a thousand years, once again the people of Moses entered the Holy Land. The State of Israel was created. That too was a return. But as it was celebrated by Schönberg in his cantata, it was not the return of man towards God, it was the return of God towards man: *Gottes Wiederkehr.* Thus, Schönberg saw events come full circle. If he, like Moses, did not enter the Land, at least he knew that God had returned to His people. The spark of light scattered to the winds had been regathered. The one who gathered it, this time, was no longer man but God. By his *teshuva*, Schönberg had become a co-worker with God.

MOUNT NEBO

Arnold Schönberg's *teshuva* reached a climax unique of its kind in the very last weeks of his life, between the month of April and July 13, 1951. That day, death surprised him in the course of a physical illness which had sapped his strength for years, and at the same time, in the midst of an ethical drama which had been enacted on two levels for several months.

There was the vertical drama of the unremitting search for an impossible dialogue with God.

There was the horizontal drama of an equally unremitting search for an impossible *aliyah* to Jerusalem.

It was as if God had issued Schönberg a call from above and one from "over there," a sign of the heavens and a sign of the earth, and as if God had cut him short at the very moment when the signs were about to be interpreted. Like Moses, Schönberg died in the intensity of an unfinished prayer. He believed he had finally obtained the fulfillment of the promise of heaven and that of the earth. Physically, his eyes were almost blinded. Spiritually, they were blinded by the Light. Was the power of the spirit, rousing itself, able to overcome the frailty of matter? Would it be able to bring this drama in two dimensions to its conclusion?

He had just finished a musical transposition of Psalm 130: *De profundis (Mi ma'amakim)*. This was opus 50b of his work. The music was his, but the words, from the Bible, were God's.

Would he be able to finish composing opus 50c, in the writing of which he had made such great strides since April? This was *Modern Psalms*. The music, once again, was his, but this time, the words also.

This was a daring project which Schönberg had been considering for forty years, since *Jacob's Ladder*. He had just finished the "Promethean" part of it. A man had dared, in the twentieth century, to take up the challenge of the ancient language and to put it in modern language. The text was already complete, a sober yet powerful incantation. A seizing upon the distant God who nevertheless was brought close by prayer. The dizzying void between the creature and the creator over which prayer nevertheless threw a bridge.

The man-written text was now completed. The Bible contains 150 psalms. Schönberg had the audacity to give the first psalm he now created the number 151. The music, however, did not keep pace with his creativity: The musical text did not go beyond the eighty-sixth bar of the first psalm.

The last chord, composed on the eve of his death, accompanied the four words which supported these unfinished prayers: "And nevertheless I pray . . ."

"Oh Thou my God, all peoples praise Thee and assure Thee of their veneration, but what can it mean to Thee whether I too do so or not?

Who am I to believe that my prayer is necessary?

When I say 'God,' I know that I am speaking of the Only, Eternal, Omnipotent, Omniscient, and Unimaginable, of whom I neither can nor should make an image. Of whom I have neither the right nor the possibility of making a demand, and who can answer my most fervent prayer or disregard it.

And nevertheless I pray, as all that lives prays, and yet I beg that I may receive forgiveness, wonders, and plenitude.

And nevertheless I pray, for I do not wish to be deprived of the happiness afforded by the sense of unity, of union with Thee, O Thou my God. Thy grace has given us prayer as a link with Thee, a link which brings blessedness, like a rapture which gives us more than any fulfillment. . . ."

As an end-scene to his life, this inner aspect of the drama would be moving enough in itself. But the outer aspect adds to it: another uncompleted dialogue, cut short by death. Now it was no longer the dialogue between Schönberg and God, but the dialogue between Schönberg and the Land of God.

This too was a forty-year-old dialogue, since Schönberg's Zionism had its roots in the years when he was working on *Jacob's Ladder*. We have traced the fluctuations of this Zionism and tried to understand them.

But suddenly, in April 1951, there was an unexpected development: "For forty years," wrote Schönberg, "it has been my most ardent desire to live as a free citizen in an independent State of Israel." This State of Israel had now been in existence for three years. Schönberg had celebrated its appearance with his cantata *Three Times A Thousand Years*.

Now, in April 1951, it was no longer a matter of writing but of action. Not words or sounds: an act—*aliyah* to Israel. That is what was offered to Schönberg, the projection of his Zionist dream into the Israeli reality.

Things, however, were not quite as simple as they appear in certain biographies of Schönberg. There are, moreover, in certain works on Schönberg and in the volume of his letters (published in Mainz in 1970 and all-important for chronological dating), contradictions, inaccuracies, and (possibly deliberate) omissions which confuse the facts which need to be clearly

established, for only clarity will enable them to be seen as constituting a
rapid and moving drama.

In 1951 two eminent figures were the moving spirits of the musical life of the young State of Israel: Frank Pelleg (1910–1968) at the
Ministry of Education and Culture, and Oedoen Partos (1907–1977) at
that time Director of the Academy of Music (or national conservatory)
which had recently been set up in Jerusalem. When the two of them had
come to Palestine around the years 1936–38, they had begun their careers
with the Israel Philharmonic, founded by Bronislav Hubermann. The idea
of this orchestra had been put forward, as we may recall, by Schönberg in
1933.

Pelleg and Partos now in 1951 offered Arnold Schönberg the post of
Honorary President of the Academy of Music.

This was the context of two of Arnold Schönberg's letters, one dated
April 26 and the other June 15. It is important not to obscure or distort the
true intention of either of them.

The offer that had been made to him filled Schönberg with pride and
joy. He did, however, have one reservation, but that did not concern the
offer in itself. What he rejected was the honorific nature of the title. He
was willing to accept the post only on one condition: That the presidency
he was offered would be effective. He did not wish to give only his name to
Jerusalem, but also himself. Arnold Schönberg in Jerusalem was not to be a
mere symbol but the realization of something he had aspired to for so
long—aliyah. His aim, he said in the letter of April 26, was to live in
Jerusalem and to work there for the creation of a generation of artists who
would be "true priests of art, who would struggle for art with the same
seriousness as the priests of God in ancient Israel. For if God has elected
the people of Israel to maintain the true monotheism of Moses in its integrity despite all persecutions and all sufferings, it is the duty of Jewish musicians to endow the world with an undertaking which will enable us once
more to manifest ourselves in a universally significant manner."

Thus, in this letter, Schönberg gave free rein to his dream of finally
becoming what he aspired to be: namely, the Master of a generation of
Jewish artists in Israel devoted to the service of the biblical message. He
added a few practical details such as the hope that his archives would be
acquired by the Israel National Library (this hope has not so far been realized: Schönberg's archives are still in Los Angeles), and the hope, also,
that the illness that was sapping him would not prevent his dream from
becoming a reality.

Schönberg had confided all this to friends in Los Angeles before re-
plying to Pelleg and Partos's official letter. The latter, having no doubt been
provided with some muddled information by Schönberg's confidants, had in

May organized a ceremony in Jerusalem in which the nomination of Arnold Schönberg to the honorary presidency had been announced.

They now hastened to write to Schönberg that of course they would be only too delighted with the Master's *aliyah* and his effective presidency of the Academy of Music. While waiting for Schönberg to be physically capable of making his *aliyah*, they asked him to send them a program from America just as he would have done if he were effectively head of the Academy.

Arnold Schönberg drew up this program on June 15th, one month before his death, in a further letter which was more than a program. It was a confession, a credo, or rather, it was a *viddui*, an *ani ma'amin*, which are corresponding Hebrew expressions more suitable to describe the Jewish character of this text. With nobility, and with a pride stemming from his certitude of have brought about a revolution in art, Schönberg reverted in this letter to the sources of his struggle for a Jewish art. There could be no art, he claimed, which was not inspired by ethics, and there could be no human ethics not inspired by the spirit of Judaism. But Schönberg had not only struggled with ideas: He had also fought with men, and, to his great misfortune, the Jews among those men who followed him were small in numbers, reticent, and sometimes opposed to him. Now Schönberg wanted to implant his message in the minds of the Israeli Jews. He therefore asked to be heard, and he asked to be given the means to make himself heard, for he was sure of his calling and his inspiration. He claimed that there were two aspects to art: spirit and technique. The younger generation in Israel should be free to learn all the techniques in the world! But the spirit was one, and that was the unique spirit of Israel of which, at the time of writing, Schönberg knew himself to be one of the rare prophets, if not the only one, in the area of art.

One should imagine that as Arnold Schönberg wrote these lines, on his working table next to this letter were the psalms he had recently written and for whose harsh accompanying sounds he was searching. In this *Ani ma'amin*, however, he struck a different chord: that of the fidelity of the Jewish people to its teachers, the renunciation of idols, the renewal of the Covenant between Israel and the Bible, a renewal which the creation of the State of Israel had graven in the granite of history. One senses in Schönberg the anger of Moses (with whom he had often identified himself) and his struggle to form a people in conformity with the ideal of the Law. Before the Land whose gates were now opening before him, he paused for a moment and took stock of the situation.

Schönberg's psalms spoke of the risks of prayer. Nothing whatsoever can compel God to answer: "And nevertheless I pray."

Schönberg's *Ani ma'amin* program spoke of the risks of the ideal.

Nothing whatsoever can compel the real to correspond to the ideal. And nevertheless I see . . .

The two "and neverthelesses" came to an end on the same day. While the letter-program was still on its way to its recipients in Jerusalem, they received the following telegram from Los Angeles: "13 July 1951, Arnold Schönberg passed away."

Arnold Schönberg's *teshuva* finally came to its resting place: Mount Nebo.

13

Kol Nidre

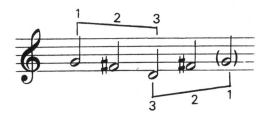

An upturned tree whose roots are in the heavens, the *ba'al teshuva* shakes with a movement that passes from the root to the top and, again, from the top to the root. Outstretched between time and eternity, between exile and the Land, between the source and the estuary, he gathers up in his dynamic the mass of contradictions and offers them up to the Unity.

On October 4, 1938, at the solemn moment of the first instants of Yom Kippur, the *ba'al teshuva* Arnold Schönberg achieved a unity between his life and art, as well as a unity, to which he had always aspired, between tradition and creativity. In one of the synagogues of Los Angeles, he himself directed the Kol Nidre with an intense fervor, which he communicated to the congregation. It was a climactic moment. In March of that year, Hitler-Amalek had carried out the *Anschluss* in Austria. The Nazis entered Vienna, where Schönberg was born, and Vienna gave itself up to the Nazis without resistance in a demoniacal delirium of Evil. In September, accords were signed in Munich where Schönberg had spent his adolescence. These accords, it was felt, would deliver up Czechoslovakia and Prague to the devil. The infernal circle was closing in around the Jews of Europe. Then, just as Beethoven had once sung his ''Ode to Joy'' in the midst of his suffering, so Schönberg, in his despair, celebrated his ''Ode to Teshuva.'' On the basis of the traditional text and melody, he created a new Kol Nidre, giving it its place not in a concert hall, but in the synagogue.

Thus, in creating, on a traditional basis, a new Kol Nidre which he hoped would find its place not in the programs of concerts but in synagogues at the solemn moment of the first instants of Yom Kippur, Arnold Schönberg willingly divested himself of the garment in which art, academism, and culture had clothed him in order to return to the condition of a simple *paytan*, an inspired liturgist, a poet of God, of whom there had been so many in the synagogues of the Middle Ages, a Levitical psalmist such as had been found within the walls of the Temple when it stood in Jerusalem.

This was the gesture of the creature divesting himself before the creator, of putting on the *sargueness* or *kittel*, the mortuary costume in which the congregants had clothed themselves, and which had made such a strong impression on Franz Rosenzweig when he entered the Berlin synagogue on the eve of Kol Nidre.

But this was also the gesture of the High Priest divesting himself for the Yom Kippur service in the Temple when it stood in Jerusalem. Throughout the entire year, the High Priest officiated in a magnificent ceremonial costume adorned with precious stones, gilding, bells, and pomegranates. On Yom Kippur, he entered the Holy of Holies in a white vestment without adornment similar to the *kittel* or *sargueness* which after the fall of the Temple each simple Jew was to put on, in some way substituting himself for the High Priest in his *avodah*, in a symbolic and vicarious service.

It was this vicarious role which was now assumed by Arnold Schönberg.

If I have not spoken so far of Kol Nidre in my account of Schönberg's work, it is because I wish to reserve my discussion of it for the end of this book, for here Schönberg was the representative of *teshuva* as such. He apprehended the two essential forms of it.

First, the form created by the "anti." The preparatory notes written by Schönberg in the summer of 1938 show that the Kol Nidre intended for Yom Kippur in October of that year resulted from the shocks of the *Anschluss* and the Sudetenland affair. The "four points" of the program of 1933 once more made their appearance. Once again, Schönberg dreamed of a form of Jewish politics strong enough to oppose on its own the force of the "anti." Arnold Schönberg's Kol Nidre was a reflection of the physical force of the Jewish people.

But it was also obviously a reflection of the force resulting from the "meta"—the "meta" which had been at work in Schönberg since his awakening to Judaism and to God. Arnold Schönberg's Kol Nidre was thus also the reflection of the moral and religious power of the Jewish community.

A Kol Nidre representing a synthesis. How could it have been otherwise?

Kol Nidre is indeed the most significant prayer of Jewish *teshuva,* since it begins the twenty-four hours of Yom Kippur in all the synagogues in the world, full to bursting point. Its archaic, hermetic Aramaic text seems to be hewn out of the rock of the incomprehensible, and yet every Jew accepts it as if it had been especially written for him, for him personally, for his return into the heart of the community even if it is only for

these twenty-four hours, and even if, during the whole year, he was separated and alienated from it.

This text is accompanied by a melody—breathless, rhythmic, un-
even—concerning which one may say what Heine said of the Passover Haggada: that it moves one to the depths of one's being. No Jew can resist its
enchantment. This is no doubt because it originated with the Marranos,
those clandestine returners whose heart was torn between public conversion
to Christianity or to Islam and secret fidelity to Jewish existence. Torn between appearance and reality, this melody lays bare an abyss. It tears away
the veil, snatches off the mask, restores the Jew to the naked truth, and this
is what the mysterious words of Kol Nidre seek to express—namely, that
no vow, no commitment, no oath, no wager can hold when one is face-
to-face with God.

Arnold Schönberg's contribution to the Kol Nidre was twofold. Without exceeding the time span of twenty minutes which the traditional liturgy
allows for this introduction to Yom Kippur, and without altering either the
sub-stratum of the melody nor the purpose of the text, he pulverized the
one—or rather, to use his own expression, he "vitriolized" it—and amplified the other by placing the tragedy of the Jewish soul within the drama of
the divine cosmos.

For such had been the popularity of the melody of Kol Nidre that,
before Schönberg, dozens of musicians, Jews and non-Jews, had detached it
from its liturgical context of Yom Kippur in order to make it into a concert
piece. The most famous adaptation, that of Max Bruch, a non-Jew, figured
on the program of soirées where the violin was supposed to draw tears from
the public, together with Chopin's *Marche Funèbre* and Brahms's *Slow
Waltzes*. For Schönberg, this was worse than sacreligious: it was "senti-
mentality." What he wanted to do in re-composing the melody of Kol Nidre
was, he said, to "confer on this edict the dignity of a law."

"I think I succeeded in this," he was able to say with some pride.
The success lay in his discovery of the mathematics underlying the traditional theme of Kol Nidre. This schema utilized the same notes in its upsurge and its regression. It was sufficient to combine this reciprocal
movement of rising and falling, falling and rising, in order to suggest the
dignity of the law of Returning, of *teshuva*.

The general intention of this law was further emphasized by a simple
but poignant modification of the traditional rhythm. It begins very softly,
increases in volume and ends very loudly, the whole of Kol Nidre being
repeated at a corresponding level of musical intensity. Schönberg, however,
gives the Kol Nidre only one hearing, and he begins with a burst of thunder
and concludes very softly, with a thin drawn-out murmur. It is the brutal
shock of a solitary person suddenly being taken hold of, which eases off

into the modest intimacy of a dialogue. God first takes hold of man and then He talks to him.

If the musical treatment takes the form of a dialogue, that is because the text of Kol Nidre was transformed by Schönberg into a dialogue. His version is a work for solo voice or cantor, choir, and orchestra. The cantor, who is the rabbi, begins his recitation with words recalling a legend of the Cabbala: that of the stars which were lost in the course of the creation. It is an amplification of the verse with which Kol Nidre begins in the liturgy of the synagogue: *Or zarua la-tsaddik,* light is sown for the righteous. But the Cabbala modifies this idea: Light is sown for the righteous, but also for the returner. As much as, or even more than the righteous, the *ba'al teshuva* is a tracer of the lost light. This light he not only restores to himself but to the whole universe. From the nothingness in which he had been in danger of losing himself, the *ba'al teshuva* brings the spark back to God. Thus, anyone who refashions his own soul refashions the soul of the Universe.

What better conclusion could I have found to my book than the introduction of the *ba'al teshuva* Arnold Schönberg to the Kol Nidre of Jewish *teshuva?*

Rabbi: The Cabbala relates a legend. In the beginning, God said: 'Let there be light!' From infinite space a flame sprang up. God scattered this light into atoms. Myriad sparks were hidden in the universe, but not all of us can perceive them. The vain man who walks proudly will never notice them, but the modest and humble man whose eyes are lowered is able to see them. 'A light has been sown for the righteous.'

Bi-shivoh shel maloh u-vishivoh shel matoh.

In the name of God, we solemnly urge that every transgressor, even if unfaithful to our people out of fear or led astray by false doctrines of any kind, be liberated from his weakness or his greed. We invite him to unite himself with us in prayer tonight. A light has been sown for the righteous—a light has been sown for the *ba'al teshuva.*

Choir: KOL NIDRE

A light has been sown for the *ba'al teshuva.*

Rabbi: We invite him to be one of us tonight.

Choir: *Teshuva.*

We make our souls anew . . . Kol Nidre . . .

GLOSSARY OF HEBREW TERMS

Ani ma'min ("I believe"): a traditional formula introducing a statement of belief.

Avodah: this word signifies both work and prayer.

Ba'al teshuva: see the introductory quotation to this book. It can only be rendered by a circumlocution, e.g.: "someone who refashions his soul." Plural: *ba'alei teshuva.*

Be'emtsa: in the middle or diagonally. A term taken from the Maharal of Prague (16th century).

Bereshit: "In the beginning," the opening words of the Bible.

Brit: alliance, covenant.

Boher: rabbinic student.

Eretz Israel: the Land of Israel.

Kashrut: dietary laws.

Shabbat: Saturday, the sacred day of rest.

Had Gadya: the poem ending the ritual of the Haggada on Seder night.

Haganah: defense organization of the Jewish community in Mandatory Palestine.

Haggadah: the text read at the Seder ceremony on Passover eve.

Halutz: Zionist pioneer in Eretz Israel.

Havdalah: ceremony ending the Sabbath.

Kaddish: a prayer of sanctification said in memory of a deceased person.

Kippur: a day of repentance and fasting held on the 10th of Tishri in the Jewish calendar.

Kol Nidre: the prayer beginning the Yom Kippur service.

Meforshim: the traditional commentators.

Minha: the late afternoon prayers.

Mitzva: commandment. Plural: *mitzvot.*

Nazir: Nazarite. Person dedicated to God (see Numbers 6).

Ne'ila: prayers ending the Yom Kippur service.

Pesach: Passover.

Plugto: point of controversy.

Rav: rabbi.

Rehem: womb.

Rosh Hashana: the New Year.

Seder: family celebration on Passover night commemorating the Exodus from Egypt.

Shoa: the genocide of six million Jews under the Third Reich. This Hebrew term is very badly rendered by the usual translation, "Holocaust."

Tallith: prayer shawl.

Tefillin: phalacteries.

Tishri: a month of the Jewish year, in autumn.

Torah: the Pentateuch, the five books or Law of Moses. The oral Torah is the Talmud and the rabbinic literature including the Aggada and the Midrash.

Tsaddik: a righteous man.

Viddui: confession of sins on Yom Kippur.

Yom Kippur: the day of *kippur* (see *kippur*).

Zuz, plural *zuzim:*   small coinage.

SHORT BIBLIOGRAPHY

Bibliographical portraits of the writers mentioned at the beginning of this book in "Opening Chords" (in the order of their presentation).

HEINRICH HEINE

Complete Works, Hamburg, 1887.
Mein wertvollstes Vermächtnis, Zurich, 1950. An excellent anthology of his Jewish writings by Felix Stössinger.
Ross, W., *Heinrich Heine, Two Studies of His Thought and Feeling.* 1956.

BERNARD LAZARE

Job's Dungheap, New York, 1948, with a portrait of Bernard Lazare by Charles Péguy.
Wilson, Nelly, *Bernard Lazare,* Cambridge University Press, 1978.

FRANZ ROSENZWEIG

The Star of Redemption, London, 1971.
Glatzer, Nahum N., *Franz Rosenzweig, His Life and Thought,* Philadelphia, 1953.
Neher, André, "Une approche théologique et sociologique de la relation judeo-chrétienne: le dialogue Franz Rosenzweig–Eugen Rosenstock", in *L'Existence juive,* Paris, 1976, p. 212 ff., with a bibliography.

ARNOLD SCHÖNBERG

Works (a complete list, including the libretti and the political texts may be found in Rufer, Josef, *Das Werk Arnold Schönbergs,* New York, 1959, and Stein, L., ed., *Ausgewählte Briefe,* Mainz, 1958).
Arnold Schönberg Archives, Belmont, Los Angeles.

Schönberg dossier, Georg Alter Archives, National Library, Jerusalem.
Journal of the Arnold Schönberg Institute, Los Angeles, from October, 1976.
MacDonald, Malcolm, *Schoenberg*, London, 1976.
Payne, Anthony, *Schoenberg*, London, Oxford University Press, 1968.
Reich, Willi, *Schoenberg, a Critical Biography*, New York, 1971.
Stuckenschmidt, Hans, *Schönberg*, Zurich, 1974.

KARL WOLFSKEHL

Gesammelte Werke, two volumes, Hamburg, 1960 (complete works, edited by Margot Ruben and Claus Victor Bock).
So far, there exists no general study of Wolfskehl, and no translation into the English language except for *1933, A Poem Sequence* (a translation of *Die Stimme Spricht*), New York, c.1947.

BENJAMIN FONDANE

L'Exode, Super Flumina Babylonis, preface by Claude Sernet, Paris, 1965.
"Benjamin Fondane", in the review *Non Lieu*, Paris, 1978 (with bibliography, pp. 194–195).

AARON ABRAHAM KABAK

Shlomo Molko, Tel-Aviv, 1929. (In English, *Shelomo Molho*, Tel Aviv, 1973).
Bemishol Hatsar, Tel-Aviv, 1935. (In English, *The Narrow Path, the Man of Nazareth*, Tel Aviv, 1968).
Halkin, Simon, *Modern Hebrew Literature*, New York, 1950.
Wallenrod, R., *The Literature of Modern Israel*, New York, 1956.

DAVID COHEN (Rav Hanazir)

Kol Hanevua, Jerusalem, 1972.

INDEX

CATHOLIC THEOLOGICAL UNION

3 0311 00120 3095

BM 565 .N4413 1990
Neher, Andrâe.
They made their souls anew